JAVASCRIPT
INTERVIEW QUESTIONS
AND
ANSWERS

50 Essential Questions to Ace Coding Interviews

MAXWELL RIVERS

Copyright © 2023 Maxwell Rivers

All rights reserved.

INTRODUCTION

Welcome to "Python: Interview Questions and Answers." Whether you are a seasoned Python developer looking to brush up on your interview skills or a newcomer aiming to break into the exciting world of Python programming, this book is designed to be your essential companion.

Python has emerged as one of the most popular and versatile programming languages in recent years. Its simplicity, readability, and a vast ecosystem of libraries and frameworks have made it a top choice for a wide range of applications, from web development and data analysis to machine learning and automation. As a result, Python skills are in high demand, and job opportunities for Python developers are abundant.

If you're on the journey to secure your dream job or simply want to enhance your Python knowledge, mastering the art of Python interviews is crucial. This book has been meticulously crafted to equip you with the knowledge and confidence needed to excel in Python interviews of all kinds, whether for entry-level positions or senior roles.

How to Use This Book

This book is divided into ten comprehensive chapters, each focusing on specific aspects of Python programming and related interview questions. Each chapter contains a collection of carefully selected questions that are commonly asked during Python interviews. We've provided detailed, insightful answers to these questions to help you not only understand the concepts but also communicate your knowledge effectively during interviews.

For the best learning experience, we recommend the following approach:

1. **Read and Understand**: Start by reading each question thoroughly to grasp its context and intent. Try to answer the question on your own before referring to our answers.

2. **Explore the Answers**: After attempting to answer the question, review our comprehensive answers. These answers provide clear explanations, examples, and insights that will deepen your understanding of the topic.

3. **Practice and Reinforce**: Reinforce your learning by

practicing the code examples and exercises provided throughout the book. Hands-on experience is invaluable when preparing for interviews.

4. **Customize Your Study Plan**: Depending on your experience and interview goals, you can customize your study plan. Focus on the chapters and questions that align with your specific needs.

5. **Stay Updated**: The field of Python programming is dynamic, with new libraries and best practices emerging regularly. While this book provides a strong foundation, it's essential to stay updated with the latest trends and developments in the Python ecosystem.

Remember that interview success isn't just about answering questions correctly; it's also about demonstrating your problem-solving abilities, your passion for Python, and your ability to work effectively as part of a team.

Whether you're aiming for your first Python role or striving for a more senior position, this book will be your trusted companion on your path to success.

Best of luck with your Python interviews!

CONTENTS

PYTHON BASICS

What is Python, and why is it popular for programming?

Python is a high-level, interpreted programming language known for its simplicity, versatility, and readability. It has gained immense popularity in the world of programming for several compelling reasons:

1. **Ease of Learning and Readability**: Python's syntax is clear and easy to read, resembling plain English. This makes it an excellent choice for beginners and experienced programmers alike. Python's simplicity reduces the learning curve and allows developers to focus on problem-solving rather than deciphering complex code.

2. **Versatility**: Python is a general-purpose language, meaning it can be used for a wide range of applications. It's commonly used in web development, data analysis, scientific computing, artificial intelligence, machine learning, automation, and more. Its versatility makes it a go-to language for various domains.

3. **Large Standard Library**: Python comes with a comprehensive standard library that includes a wide range of modules and packages. These built-in tools simplify common programming tasks, saving developers time and effort. It also promotes code reuse and consistency.

4. **Active and Supportive Community**: Python has a large and

active community of developers who contribute to its growth and development. This community support means you can find ample resources, tutorials, and third-party libraries to extend Python's functionality.

5. **Cross-Platform Compatibility**: Python is available on various operating systems, including Windows, macOS, and Linux. This cross-platform compatibility ensures that Python applications can run seamlessly on different environments.

6. **Open Source**: Python is open-source, meaning it's freely available for anyone to use and modify. This encourages collaboration and innovation, leading to a wealth of open-source projects and tools.

7. **Strong in Data Science and Machine Learning**: Python has become the preferred language for data science and machine learning due to libraries like NumPy, pandas, Matplotlib, and TensorFlow. Its simplicity and powerful libraries make it an ideal choice for data analysis and modeling.

8. **Integration Capabilities**: Python can easily integrate with other languages like C, C++, and Java, allowing developers to leverage existing code and libraries written in those languages.

9. **Extensibility**: Python can be extended using C or C++ code, making it suitable for performance-critical applications while retaining its high-level ease of use.

10. **Wide Industry Adoption**: Many large tech companies, including Google, Dropbox, Instagram, and NASA, use Python for various aspects of their projects, further cementing its popularity and relevance in the industry.

Explain the difference between Python 2 and Python 3.

Python 2 and Python 3 are two distinct versions of the Python programming language. While they share many similarities, there are also significant differences between them:

1. **Print Statement vs. Print Function:**
   - **Python 2:** In Python 2, the "print" statement is used to display output. For example: **print "Hello, World!"**.
   - **Python 3:** Python 3 replaces the "print" statement with a "print" function, which requires parentheses. For example:

print("Hello, World!"). This change improves consistency and compatibility with other functions.

2. **Integer Division:**
   - **Python 2:** Integer division using the "/" operator truncates the decimal part, resulting in an integer. For example, **5 / 2** equals **2**.
   - **Python 3:** In Python 3, "/" performs true division, retaining the decimal part. To achieve integer division, you use "//." For example, **5 / 2** equals **2.5**, while **5 // 2** equals **2**.

3. **Unicode Strings:**
   - **Python 2:** Strings are represented as ASCII by default. To work with Unicode, you need to use the "u" prefix or the "unicode" function explicitly.
   - **Python 3:** Strings are Unicode by default. To represent bytes, you use the "b" prefix for byte literals.

4. **Iterating Over Dictionaries:**
   - **Python 2:** In Python 2, iterating over a dictionary using a "for" loop would return keys by default. To iterate over values, you need to use the ".values()" method explicitly.
   - **Python 3:** In Python 3, dictionary iteration directly returns keys by default, which aligns with the Pythonic principle of "explicit is better than implicit." To iterate over values, you can still use ".values()" explicitly.

5. **Range vs. xrange:**
   - **Python 2:** Python 2 includes both the "range" function and the more memory-efficient "xrange" function for creating sequences of numbers. "xrange" is preferred for large ranges.
   - **Python 3:** Python 3 eliminates "xrange" and uses the more efficient "range" behavior by default. The original "range" in Python 2 behaves like "xrange" in Python 3.

6. **Input Function:**
   - **Python 2:** The "input()" function in Python 2 evaluates the input as a Python expression. To get user input as a string, you should use "raw_input()" instead.
   - **Python 3:** In Python 3, "input()" returns a string, making it safer for user input. The previous behavior of "input()" in Python 2 is equivalent to "eval(input())" in Python 3.

7. **Exceptions:**
   - **Python 2:** In Python 2, exceptions are typically defined using

a tuple, such as **except Exception, e:**. This syntax is replaced in Python 3 with **except Exception as e:** for improved clarity.

8. **Function Annotations:**
   - **Python 2:** Python 2 does not support function annotations, which allow you to add metadata to function arguments and return values.
   - **Python 3:** Python 3 introduces support for function annotations, enhancing code readability and documentation.
9. **Bytes and Strings Separation:**
   - **Python 2:** Python 2 does not clearly distinguish between bytes and text strings, which can lead to encoding/decoding issues.
   - **Python 3:** Python 3 enforces a clear separation between bytes and text strings, reducing ambiguity and encoding-related errors.

Python 2 reached its end of life on January 1, 2020, and is no longer receiving updates or support. It is highly recommended to use Python 3 for all new projects and to migrate existing Python 2 code to Python 3 to take advantage of the language's improvements and ongoing support.

How do you install Python on different platforms?

Python can be installed on various platforms, including Windows, macOS, and Linux. Here's a general guide on how to install Python on these different platforms:

1. Installing Python on Windows:
- Visit the official Python website at https://www.python.org/downloads/windows/.
- Download the latest Python installer for Windows, which is available as an executable (.exe) installer.
- Run the downloaded installer.
- Check the box that says "Add Python x.x to PATH" during installation. This step is essential for running Python from the command line.
- Follow the installation wizard's instructions, and Python will be installed on your Windows system.

2. Installing Python on macOS:

- macOS typically comes with Python preinstalled, but it might be an older version. You can install a newer version using package managers like Homebrew or manually as follows:
  - Using Homebrew (recommended):
    - Install Homebrew if you haven't already by following the instructions on https://brew.sh/.
    - Open Terminal and run the command: **brew install python**.
  - This will install Python 3.x, and you can access it using the **python3** command.
- Manual Installation:
    - Visit the official Python website at https://www.python.org/downloads/macos/.
    - Download the macOS installer for the desired Python version.
  - Run the downloaded installer and follow the on-screen instructions.

3. Installing Python on Linux:

- Most Linux distributions come with Python preinstalled. You can check the installed version using the command: **python --version** or **python3 --version**.
- To install or update Python on Linux, you can use your distribution's package manager. For example:
  - On Ubuntu/Debian-based systems:
    - Open Terminal and run: **sudo apt-get update**
    - Install Python 3 with: **sudo apt-get install python3**
  - On CentOS/Fedora-based systems:
    - Open Terminal and run: **sudo yum update**
    - Install Python 3 with: **sudo yum install python3**
  - On Arch Linux:
    - Open Terminal and run: **sudo pacman -Syu**
    - Install Python 3 with: **sudo pacman -S python**
- To install additional Python packages and libraries, you can use the package manager or Python's package manager, **pip**. For example, to install **pip**, use: **sudo apt-get install python3-pip** on Ubuntu.

Remember that Python has two major versions in common use: Python 2.x and Python 3.x. Python 2 is no longer supported, so it's recommended to use Python 3 for all new projects. Depending on your system and configuration, you may need to use **python3** instead of **python** to run Python 3.x specifically.

What are the main characteristics of Python as a programming language?

Python is a widely used and versatile programming language known for its unique set of characteristics that make it popular among developers. Here are the main characteristics of Python as a programming language:

1. **Readability:** Python's syntax is simple and easy to read, emphasizing code readability. This makes it an excellent choice for both beginners and experienced developers, as it reduces the likelihood of errors and enhances collaboration.

2. **Simplicity:** Python's straightforward and clean syntax minimizes the use of symbols and special characters, making code more understandable. The "Zen of Python" (PEP 20) encapsulates Python's simplicity and readability principles.

3. **High-Level Language:** Python is a high-level programming language, which means it abstracts complex low-level details like memory management and hardware interactions. This abstraction allows developers to focus on solving problems rather than managing technical intricacies.

4. **Interpreted:** Python is an interpreted language, meaning that code is executed line by line by the Python interpreter. This provides an interactive and exploratory coding experience, making it easier to debug and test code.

5. **Dynamic Typing:** Python uses dynamic typing, allowing variables to change types at runtime. This flexibility simplifies code development but requires careful consideration to prevent unexpected behavior.

6. **Multi-Paradigm:** Python supports multiple programming paradigms, including procedural, object-oriented, and functional programming. Developers can choose the paradigm that best suits their project's requirements.

7. **Large Standard Library:** Python comes with a comprehensive standard library that provides modules and packages for a wide range of tasks, from file handling to web development. This

extensive library reduces the need to write code from scratch and promotes code reuse.

8. **Community and Ecosystem:** Python has a vibrant and active community of developers, resulting in a vast ecosystem of third-party libraries and frameworks. This ecosystem supports a wide variety of applications, including web development (Django, Flask), data analysis (pandas, NumPy), and machine learning (TensorFlow, PyTorch).

9. **Cross-Platform Compatibility:** Python is available on various operating systems, including Windows, macOS, and Linux. This cross-platform compatibility allows developers to create applications that run seamlessly on different environments.

10. **Open Source:** Python is an open-source language, meaning it is freely available for anyone to use, modify, and distribute. This openness encourages collaboration, innovation, and the development of a global community.

11. **Strong Community Support:** The Python community is known for its friendliness and willingness to help. Online forums, mailing lists, and communities like Stack Overflow provide valuable resources for developers seeking assistance.

12. **Extensibility:** Python can be extended using modules and libraries written in other languages, such as C or C++. This feature allows developers to optimize performance-critical parts of their code.

13. **Testing and Debugging:** Python includes built-in testing and debugging tools like the unittest and pdb modules, making it easier to write and maintain high-quality code.

14. **Web Development and Frameworks:** Python is widely used in web development, with frameworks like Django and Flask simplifying the creation of web applications, APIs, and websites.

15. **Data Science and Machine Learning:** Python's rich ecosystem of data science and machine learning libraries, including pandas, scikit-learn, and TensorFlow, has established it as a leading language in these fields.

These characteristics make Python a powerful, flexible, and accessible programming language suitable for a wide range of applications, from simple scripting tasks to complex software development and data analysis projects.

Describe the concept of Python's Global Interpreter Lock (GIL).

The Global Interpreter Lock (GIL) is a unique and often misunderstood aspect of Python's implementation that plays a crucial role in how Python manages multi-threading. Here's an explanation of the concept of Python's GIL:

1. What is the GIL?

The Global Interpreter Lock (GIL) is a mutex (mutual exclusion) that protects access to Python objects, preventing multiple native threads from executing Python bytecodes in parallel. In simpler terms, it's a lock that ensures only one thread is executing Python code at a time, even on multi-core CPUs.

2. Why Does Python Have the GIL?

Python's GIL exists primarily due to the way CPython (the reference implementation of Python) manages memory and handles thread safety. The GIL is a design choice made to simplify memory management and avoid complex low-level synchronization issues.

3. Implications of the GIL:

- **Limited Multithreading:** The GIL limits the effectiveness of multithreading in CPU-bound Python programs. While multiple threads can be created, they won't execute CPU-bound tasks in parallel because they all contend for the GIL.

- **Effective for I/O-Bound Tasks:** The GIL is less of a hindrance for I/O-bound tasks, where most of the time is spent waiting for external resources (e.g., file I/O, network requests). In such cases, Python threads can be beneficial for concurrency.

- **No Multicore Performance Boost:** The GIL prevents Python from taking full advantage of multi-core processors. This means that a Python program with threads may not perform significantly faster on a multi-core CPU compared to a single-core CPU for CPU-bound tasks.

- **Global Interpreter Lock, Not Global Locking:** The GIL doesn't prevent threads from running altogether. It only restricts the execution of Python bytecode, allowing threads to execute native (C) code and I/O operations concurrently. This is why Python threads can be suitable for I/O-bound tasks.

4. Mitigating the GIL:

- **Using Multiprocessing:** To leverage multiple cores, Python developers often use the multiprocessing module, which creates separate processes, each with its own Python interpreter and memory space. This approach avoids the GIL limitations but requires inter-process communication mechanisms.

- **Using C Extensions:** Certain performance-critical tasks can be implemented in C or C++ extensions, bypassing the GIL and achieving true parallelism.

5. GIL and Python's Memory Management:

The GIL simplifies memory management in CPython by ensuring that only one thread accesses Python objects at a time. This reduces the complexity of reference counting and garbage collection. However, it can also lead to performance bottlenecks in multi-threaded CPU-bound applications.

DATA TYPES AND VARIABLES

What are the basic data types in Python?

In Python, basic data types represent the fundamental building blocks for storing and manipulating data in your programs. Python provides several basic data types, and understanding them is essential for effective programming. Here are the most common basic data types in Python:

1. **Integers (int):**
   - Used to represent whole numbers, both positive and negative.
   - Example: **42, -10, 0**.
2. **Floating-Point Numbers (float):**
   - Used to represent real numbers with decimal points.
   - Example: **3.14, -0.001, 2.71828**.
3. **Strings (str):**
   - Used to represent text and character sequences enclosed in single, double, or triple quotes.
   - Example: **'Hello, World!', "Python", '''Multiline string'''**.
4. **Booleans (bool):**
   - Used to represent truth values, either **True** or **False**.
   - Often used in conditional statements and logical operations.
5. **Lists (list):**
   - Ordered collections of items that can be of mixed data types.
   - Enclosed in square brackets **[ ]**.
   - Example: **[1, 2, 3, 4], ['apple', 'banana', 'cherry']**.

6. **Tuples (tuple):**
    - Similar to lists but immutable, meaning their elements cannot be changed after creation.
    - Enclosed in parentheses ( ).
    - Example: **(1, 2, 3)**, **('red', 'green', 'blue')**.
7. **Dictionaries (dict):**
    - Key-value pairs that allow efficient data retrieval.
    - Enclosed in curly braces { }.
    - Example: **{'name': 'Alice', 'age': 30, 'city': 'New York'}**.
8. **Sets (set):**
    - Unordered collections of unique elements.
    - Enclosed in curly braces { } or created using the **set()** constructor.
    - Example: **{1, 2, 3}**, **{'apple', 'banana', 'cherry'}**.
9. **NoneType (None):**
    - Represents the absence of a value or a null value.
- Often used to initialize variables or indicate that a function has no return value.

Explain the difference between mutable and immutable data types.

Mutable and immutable data types in Python refer to whether an object's value can be changed (mutable) or not (immutable) after it's created. Understanding this distinction is important because it affects how you work with data in Python. Here's a detailed explanation of the difference between mutable and immutable data types:

Immutable Data Types:

1. **Immutable Definition:** Immutable objects are those whose values cannot be changed after creation. If you want to modify an immutable object, you create a new object with the desired value.
2. **Examples of Immutable Types:** Some common examples of immutable data types in Python include:
    - **int**: Integer values are immutable. For example, **x = 5** creates an integer object with the value 5. You cannot change this value; instead, you create a new integer object with a different value.
    - **float**: Floating-point numbers, like integers, are immutable.
    - **str**: Strings are immutable. For example, if you have **s =**

"Hello", you cannot change a single character in **s**. Instead, you create a new string with the desired modification.

- **tuple**: Tuples are immutable. Once you create a tuple, you cannot change its elements. If you want to modify a tuple, you create a new tuple with the desired changes.

3. **Advantages of Immutable Types:**
   - Immutability ensures data integrity and safety because once a value is set, it cannot be accidentally altered.
   - Immutable objects are hashable, making them suitable for keys in dictionaries or elements in sets.

Mutable Data Types:

1. **Mutable Definition:** Mutable objects are those whose values can be changed after creation. You can modify the content, add or remove elements, or change attributes of a mutable object without creating a new object.

2. **Examples of Mutable Types:** Some common examples of mutable data types in Python include:
   - **list**: Lists are mutable. You can change their elements, add items, or remove items without creating a new list.
   - **dict**: Dictionaries are mutable. You can add, remove, or modify key-value pairs in a dictionary.
   - **set**: Sets are mutable. You can add or remove elements from a set.
   - **custom objects**: Objects of custom classes can be mutable if you define methods that allow modification of their attributes.

3. **Advantages of Mutable Types:**
   - Mutability allows you to modify data in place, which can be more memory-efficient and faster for certain operations compared to creating new objects.

How do you declare and use variables in Python?

In Python, declaring and using variables is a fundamental aspect of programming. Variables are used to store and manipulate data in your programs. Here's how to declare and use variables in Python:

Declaring Variables:

1. **Variable Names:** Variable names in Python can consist of

letters (a-z, A-Z), digits (0-9), and underscores (_). They must start with a letter or an underscore but cannot start with a digit. Variable names are case-sensitive, so **myVar** and **myvar** are considered different variables.

2. **Assignment Operator:** To declare a variable, you use the assignment operator (=). You specify the variable name on the left side of the equal sign and the initial value on the right side.

3. **Data Type:** In Python, you don't need to explicitly declare a variable's data type; it's dynamically determined based on the assigned value. Python infers the data type automatically.

Examples of Declaring Variables:

```python
# Integer variable
age = 25

# String variable
name = "Alice"

# Floating-point variable
temperature = 98.6

# Boolean variable
is_student = True
```

Using Variables:

Once you've declared variables, you can use them throughout your code. Here are some common operations:

1. **Printing Variable Values:** You can display the value of a variable using the **print()** function.

```python
print(age)  # Prints the value of the 'age' variable
print(name)  # Prints the value of the 'name' variable
```

2. **Arithmetic Operations:** You can perform arithmetic operations with numeric variables.

```python
x = 5
y = 3
```

```
sum_result = x + y  # Adds 'x' and 'y' and stores the result in
'sum_result'
```

3. **String Manipulation:** For string variables, you can perform various operations like concatenation and slicing.

```
greeting = "Hello, "
target = "World!"
message = greeting + target  # Concatenates 'greeting' and 'target'
into 'message'
```

4. **Conditional Statements:** Variables can be used in conditional statements like **if, elif,** and **else**.

```
if age >= 18:
    print("You are an adult.")
else:
    print("You are not yet an adult.")
```

5. **Loops:** Variables often play a role in loops, where their values change during each iteration.

```
for i in range(5):
    print(i)  # 'i' takes on values from 0 to 4 in each iteration
```

6. **Updating Variables:** You can update the value of a variable by assigning it a new value.

```
x = 5
x = x + 1  # Increases the value of 'x' by 1; 'x' is now 6
```

What is variable scope in Python?

Variable scope in Python refers to the region or context in which a variable is defined and can be accessed or modified. Python has different variable scopes, which determine where a variable is visible and what parts of your code can access it. Understanding variable scope is crucial for writing bug-free and maintainable code.

There are two main types of variable scope in Python:

1. **Local Scope:**

- Variables defined within a function are considered to have local scope.
- Local variables can only be accessed and modified within the function in which they are defined.
- They are not visible or accessible outside of the function.
- Local variables are temporary and typically exist only during the execution of the function.

```python
def my_function():
    local_var = 42  # 'local_var' has local scope
    print(local_var)


my_function()
# Accessing 'local_var' here would result in an error because it's not defined in this scope.
```

2. **Global Scope:**
   - Variables defined outside of any function or block have global scope.
   - Global variables are accessible from any part of the code, including functions.
   - They persist throughout the entire program's execution.
   - Modifying a global variable within a function requires using the **global** keyword to indicate that you want to work with the global variable, not create a new local variable with the same name.

```python
global_var = 100  # 'global_var' has global scope


def my_function():
    global global_var  # Use the 'global' keyword to indicate you're working with the global variable
    global_var += 1   # Modifying the global variable


my_function()
print(global_var)  # Outputs 101
```

Nested Scopes:
Python supports nested scopes, where variables can have both

local and enclosing (non-local) scopes. In such cases, Python searches for a variable's value first in the local scope and then in any enclosing scopes, following the **LEGB rule**:

- **Local (L)**: Search for the variable in the current local scope (inside the function).
- **Enclosing (E)**: Search for the variable in any enclosing (non-local) scopes, such as outer functions.
- **Global (G)**: Search for the variable in the global scope (outside of all functions).
- **Built-in (B)**: If the variable is not found in any of the above scopes, Python searches for it in the built-in scope, which contains Python's built-in functions and objects.

Here's an example of nested scopes:

```python
global_var = 100  # Global scope

def outer_function():
    outer_var = 42  # Enclosing scope

    def inner_function():
        local_var = 10  # Local scope
        print(local_var, outer_var, global_var)  # Accessing variables from different scopes

    inner_function()

outer_function()
```

In this example, **inner_function** has access to variables in its local scope (**local_var**), the enclosing scope (**outer_var**), and the global scope (**global_var**).

What is type casting, and how is it done in Python?

Type casting, also known as **type conversion**, is the process of converting one data type into another in a programming language. In Python, type casting allows you to change the data type of a value, variable, or expression. This is particularly useful when you need to perform operations that require operands of the same data type or when you want to represent data in a different format.

Python provides several built-in functions for type casting. Here are some common type casting functions and examples of how to use them:

1. **int()**:
    - Converts a value to an integer data type.
    - Example:

```
float_num = 3.14159
int_num = int(float_num)  # Converts the floating-point number
to an integer (3)
```

2. **float()**:
    - Converts a value to a floating-point data type.
    - Example:

```
int_num = 42
float_num = float(int_num)  # Converts the integer to a floating-
point number (42.0)
```

3. **str()**:
    - Converts a value to a string data type.
    - Example:

```
number = 123
text = str(number)  # Converts the number to a string ("123")
```

4. **list()** and **tuple()**:
    - Convert sequences (e.g., strings, lists, tuples) to lists or tuples, respectively.
    - Example:

```
my_string = "Hello"
my_list = list(my_string)  # Converts the string to a list (['H', 'e',
'l', 'l', 'o'])
my_tuple = tuple(my_list)  # Converts the list to a tuple (('H', 'e',
'l', 'l', 'o'))
```

5. **bool()**:
   - Converts a value to a Boolean data type. Most values evaluate to **True**, except for **False**, **None**, numeric zero (0), and empty sequences or containers.
   - Example:

```
number = 42
bool_value = bool(number)  # Converts the number to a Boolean
(True)
```

6. **Custom Type Casting**:
   - You can also perform custom type casting using user-defined functions or constructors for your custom classes. This allows you to define how objects of your custom types are converted to other types.

```
class MyCustomType:
    def __init__(self, value):
        self.value = value

def custom_cast(obj):
    return obj.value

custom_obj = MyCustomType(42)
int_value = int(custom_obj)  # Custom type casting using a user-
defined function
```

CONTROL FLOW

Describe Python's conditional statements (if, elif, else).

Python's conditional statements, which include the **if, elif** (short for "else if"), and **else** keywords, are essential tools for making decisions in your code. These statements allow you to control the flow of your program by executing different blocks of code based on specified conditions. Here's a detailed description of Python's conditional statements:

1. **if Statement:**
    - The **if** statement is used to evaluate a condition or expression, and if the condition is **True**, the code block following the **if** statement is executed.
    - If the condition is **False**, the code block is skipped.
  - The **if** statement is often used as the starting point for conditional logic.

```
x = 10
if x > 5:
    print("x is greater than 5")
```

2. **elif Statement:**
    - The **elif** statement is used to check an additional condition if the preceding **if** or **elif** conditions are **False**.

- You can have multiple **elif** statements following an **if** statement to check multiple conditions in sequence.
- If an **elif** condition is **True**, the corresponding code block is executed, and subsequent **elif** and **else** blocks are skipped.

```python
x = 3
if x > 5:
    print("x is greater than 5")
elif x > 0:
    print("x is positive")
```

3. **else Statement:**
   - The **else** statement is used to provide a default code block to execute when none of the preceding **if** and **elif** conditions are **True**.
   - It is optional and can appear after an **if** or a series of **elif** statements.

```python
x = -2
if x > 0:
    print("x is positive")
else:
    print("x is not positive")
```

4. **Nesting Conditional Statements:**
   - You can nest conditional statements within each other to create more complex decision-making logic.
   - Proper indentation is crucial to indicate the level of nesting.

```python
x = 10
if x > 5:
    if x % 2 == 0:
        print("x is greater than 5 and even")
    else:
        print("x is greater than 5 but not even")
```

5. **Combining Conditions:**
   - You can use logical operators such as **and, or,** and **not** to combine multiple conditions in your **if, elif,** and **else**

statements.

```
x = 7
if x > 5 and x % 2 == 0:
    print("x is greater than 5 and even")
```

Explain the concept of loops in Python (for, while).

In Python, loops are control structures that allow you to repeatedly execute a block of code as long as a certain condition is met. There are two primary types of loops in Python: **for** loops and **while** loops. These loops play a crucial role in automating repetitive tasks and iterating over data structures. Here's an explanation of both types of loops:

1. for Loops:

- **for** loops are used when you know in advance how many times you want to repeat a block of code. They are commonly used for iterating over sequences like lists, tuples, strings, or ranges.
- The **for** loop iterates over each item in the sequence, executing the code block for each item.
- Syntax:

```
for variable in sequence:
    # Code block to execute for each item in the sequence
```

- Example: Iterating over a list of numbers.

```
numbers = [1, 2, 3, 4, 5]
for num in numbers:
    print(num)
```

2. while Loops:

- **while** loops are used when you want to repeatedly execute a block of code as long as a specific condition remains **True**. They are suitable for situations where you don't know in advance how many iterations are needed.
- The loop continues to execute until the condition becomes **False**.

- Syntax:

```
while condition:
    # Code block to execute while the condition is True
```

- Example: Using a **while** loop to count down from 5 to 1.

```
count = 5
while count > 0:
    print(count)
    count -= 1
```

Loop Control Statements:
- Both **for** and **while** loops can be controlled using loop control statements:
- **break**: Terminates the loop prematurely when a specific condition is met. It exits the loop entirely.

```
for num in range(10):
    if num == 5:
        break
    print(num)  # Prints numbers 0 to 4
```

- **continue**: Skips the current iteration of the loop and proceeds to the next iteration when a specific condition is met.

```
for num in range(5):
    if num == 2:
        continue
    print(num)  # Prints numbers 0, 1, 3, 4
```

- **else** with Loops: Python allows you to use an **else** block with loops, which gets executed when the loop completes normally (i.e., without encountering a **break** statement).

```
for num in range(5):
    print(num)
else:
    print("Loop completed without encountering a break
```

statement.")

What is the purpose of the "break" and "continue" statements in loops?

In Python, the "break" and "continue" statements are loop control statements used to modify the flow of execution within loops, such as "for" and "while" loops. They serve distinct purposes in loops:

1. break Statement:

- The "break" statement is used to prematurely exit a loop when a certain condition is met. It allows you to terminate the loop before it naturally completes all iterations.
- The primary purpose of "break" is to provide an early exit from a loop when a specific condition or event occurs that makes further iterations unnecessary.
- Common use cases for "break" include:
    - Terminating a loop when a target element is found while searching through a list or sequence.
    - Stopping a loop when a certain error condition is encountered.
  - Ending a loop when a user wants to exit a program's interactive menu or interface.

```
for num in range(10):
    if num == 5:
        break  # Exit the loop when 'num' reaches 5
    print(num)
```

2. continue Statement:

- The "continue" statement is used to skip the current iteration of a loop when a specific condition is met. It allows you to bypass the remaining code within the current iteration and move to the next iteration.
- The primary purpose of "continue" is to control the flow within a loop by skipping certain iterations when they are not necessary or should be skipped based on a condition.
- Common use cases for "continue" include:
    - Skipping specific values or elements within a loop based on a condition.

- Avoiding the execution of code for certain input values during data processing.
- Handling errors or exceptional cases without terminating the entire loop.

```
for num in range(5):
    if num == 2:
        continue  # Skip iteration when 'num' is 2
    print(num)
```

How do you use "try," "except," and "finally" for exception handling?

Exception handling in Python is crucial for gracefully handling errors and exceptions that may occur during the execution of your code. Python provides a structured way to handle exceptions using the **try**, **except**, and optionally, the **finally** blocks. Here's how you use these blocks for exception handling:

1. try Block:

- The **try** block contains the code where you anticipate an exception might occur. It encloses the potentially risky code that you want to monitor for exceptions.
- If an exception occurs within the **try** block, the control immediately moves to the corresponding **except** block.
- You can have multiple **try** blocks within your code.

```
try:
    # Code that may raise an exception
except ExceptionType:
    # Code to handle the exception
```

2. except Block:

- The **except** block follows the **try** block and is used to catch and handle specific exceptions.
- You specify the type of exception you want to catch (e.g., **ZeroDivisionError**, **ValueError**, or a custom exception class).
- Multiple **except** blocks can be used to handle different types of exceptions.
- You can also catch multiple exception types in a single **except**

block by using parentheses and separating them with commas.

```
try:
    # Code that may raise an exception
except ZeroDivisionError:
    # Handle division by zero
except ValueError:
    # Handle invalid input
except (TypeError, IndexError):
    # Handle multiple exception types
```

3. finally Block (Optional):

- The **finally** block, if used, is executed regardless of whether an exception occurred or not. It ensures that certain cleanup actions are taken, such as closing files or releasing resources.
- The **finally** block is often used for cleanup tasks that must be performed whether or not an exception occurred.

```
try:
    # Code that may raise an exception
except ExceptionType:
    # Code to handle the exception
finally:
    # Code that is always executed, e.g., cleanup code
```

Example:

Here's an example that demonstrates the use of **try**, **except**, and **finally**:

```
try:
    num = int(input("Enter a number: "))
    result = 10 / num
except ZeroDivisionError:
    print("Division by zero is not allowed.")
except ValueError:
    print("Invalid input. Please enter a valid number.")
finally:
    print("Execution completed.")
```

In this example, the **try** block attempts to read a number and perform a division operation. If the user enters invalid input or attempts to divide by zero, the appropriate **except** block is executed. Finally, the **finally** block ensures that the "Execution completed" message is printed, regardless of whether an exception occurred.

What is the difference between "range" and "xrange"?

In Python 2, there were two functions for creating sequences of numbers: **range()** and **xrange()**. However, in Python 3, the **xrange()** function has been removed, and the behavior of **range()** has been optimized to be similar to **xrange()** from Python 2. Here's the difference between **range()** and **xrange()** as it applied in Python 2:

1. range():

- **range()** is a built-in function in Python 2 used to generate a sequence of numbers.
- It returns a list of numbers from a start value (inclusive) to an end value (exclusive), with an optional step value.
- The entire list of numbers is created and stored in memory, which could be memory-intensive for large ranges.

numbers = range(1, 6) # Generates a list: [1, 2, 3, 4, 5]

2. xrange():

- **xrange()** is also a built-in function in Python 2 used to generate a sequence of numbers.
- Unlike **range()**, **xrange()** returns an xrange object, which is an iterator. This means that the numbers are generated on-the-fly as you iterate over them, and the entire sequence is not stored in memory.
- **xrange()** was more memory-efficient when dealing with large ranges because it did not create a complete list of numbers.

numbers = xrange(1, 6) # Generates an xrange object

Important Note: In Python 3 and later versions, **xrange()** has been removed, and **range()** has been updated to behave like the memory-efficient **xrange()** from Python 2. This means that in Python 3, you simply use the **range()** function to generate sequences of numbers efficiently, as it returns a range object similar to what **xrange()** used to do in Python 2.

FUNCTIONS AND MODULES

What are functions, and how do you define them in Python?

Functions are named blocks of code in Python that perform a specific task or a set of related tasks. They allow you to encapsulate a sequence of statements into a reusable unit, making your code more organized, modular, and easier to maintain. Functions are a fundamental concept in programming and play a vital role in structuring Python programs.

Here's how you define and use functions in Python:

Defining a Function: In Python, you define a function using the **def** keyword followed by the function name and a pair of parentheses. The function's name should follow Python's naming conventions (letters, numbers, and underscores; no spaces). After the function name, you include a colon (:) to indicate the beginning of the function body, which is a block of indented code.

```
def greet():
    print("Hello, world!")
```

In the example above, we define a function named **greet()** that prints "Hello, world!" when called.

Calling a Function: To execute the code within a function, you call it by using its name followed by parentheses. In the case of the

greet() function, you call it like this:

```
greet() # Calls the greet() function and prints "Hello, world!"
```

Function Parameters (Arguments): Functions can accept input values called **parameters** or **arguments**. Parameters are declared within the parentheses when defining the function, and they act as placeholders for values that will be provided when the function is called. You can define multiple parameters, separated by commas.

```
def greet_with_name(name):
    print(f"Hello, {name}!")
```

```
greet_with_name("Alice")    # Calls the greet_with_name() function with the argument "Alice"
```

In the example above, the **greet_with_name()** function takes a **name** parameter and prints a greeting with the provided name.

Return Values: Functions can return values using the **return** keyword. When a function returns a value, you can assign the result to a variable or use it in expressions.

```
def add(a, b):
    result = a + b
    return result
```

```
sum_result = add(3, 5)  # Calls the add() function and assigns the result (8) to sum_result
```

In this case, the **add()** function takes two arguments (**a** and **b**) and returns their sum.

Functions are essential for breaking down complex tasks into manageable parts, promoting code reusability, and enhancing code readability. They allow you to create modular and maintainable Python programs by organizing your code into logical units that can be easily tested and reused.

Explain the difference between arguments and parameters.

In Python, "arguments" and "parameters" are related but distinct concepts used when defining and calling functions. Understanding the difference between them is important for writing and working with functions effectively:

Parameters:

- **Parameters** are variables or names declared in the function definition. They act as placeholders for values that the function expects to receive when it's called. Parameters define the input requirements for the function.

- Parameters are listed in the function's parentheses in the function definition. You can specify zero or more parameters, and each parameter is followed by a name that you use to refer to the value passed into the function.

- Parameters are essentially the function's "variables" that will store the values provided when the function is called.

Arguments:

- **Arguments** are the actual values or expressions passed to a function when it is called. Arguments are the concrete data that fulfill the input requirements defined by the function's parameters.

- Arguments are specified within the parentheses when calling a function. The number and order of the arguments must match the number and order of the parameters declared in the function definition.

- Arguments are the values that are used by the function during its execution. They can be constants, variables, or expressions.

```python
# Function definition with parameters (x and y)
def add(x, y):
    result = x + y
    return result


# Function call with arguments (3 and 5)
sum_result = add(3, 5)
```

In this example:

- **x** and **y** are parameters in the function definition.
- **3** and **5** are arguments passed to the function **add()** when it is called.

How do you return multiple values from a function?

In Python, you can return multiple values from a function using various techniques. While a function can only have one **return** statement, you can use data structures like tuples, lists, or dictionaries to bundle and return multiple values as a single entity. Here are some common methods:

Using a Tuple:

You can return multiple values as a tuple, which is an ordered and immutable sequence. Define the values you want to return within parentheses and separate them with commas.

```
def get_person_info():
    name = "Alice"
    age = 30
    location = "New York"
    return name, age, location


result = get_person_info()
print(result)  # Outputs: ('Alice', 30, 'New York')
```

To access individual values from the returned tuple, you can use indexing:

```
name, age, location = get_person_info()
print(name)     # Outputs: 'Alice'
print(age)      # Outputs: 30
print(location)  # Outputs: 'New York'
```

Using a List:

Similar to tuples, you can use a list to return multiple values. Define the values within square brackets and return the list.

```
def get_fruit_list():
```

```python
    fruits = ["apple", "banana", "cherry"]
    return fruits

result = get_fruit_list()
print(result)  # Outputs: ['apple', 'banana', 'cherry']
```

Accessing values from the returned list is done through indexing:

```python
fruits = get_fruit_list()
print(fruits[0])  # Outputs: 'apple'
print(fruits[1])  # Outputs: 'banana'
print(fruits[2])  # Outputs: 'cherry'
```

Using a Dictionary:

You can also return multiple values as key-value pairs within a dictionary. Create a dictionary and return it from the function.

```python
def get_person_info():
    info = {
        "name": "Alice",
        "age": 30,
        "location": "New York"
    }
    return info

result = get_person_info()
print(result)  # Outputs: {'name': 'Alice', 'age': 30, 'location': 'New York'}
```

Accessing values from the returned dictionary is done by specifying the keys:

```python
info = get_person_info()
print(info["name"])      # Outputs: 'Alice'
print(info["age"])       # Outputs: 30
print(info["location"])  # Outputs: 'New York'
```

These methods allow you to bundle and return multiple values effectively from a Python function. Choose the method that best suits your needs and the nature of the data you want to return. Tuples are often used when you want to return multiple values that are related and should not be modified after returning, while lists and dictionaries offer more flexibility if you anticipate needing to modify the returned data.

What is a lambda function, and when is it useful?

A **lambda function** in Python is a small, anonymous function defined using the **lambda** keyword. Lambda functions are also known as **anonymous functions** because they don't have a name like regular functions defined with the **def** keyword. Instead, lambda functions are typically used for short, simple operations where creating a full-fledged named function would be overkill.

The syntax of a lambda function is as follows:

```
lambda arguments: expression
```

- **arguments** are the input parameters that the lambda function can take.
- **expression** is a single expression that the lambda function evaluates and returns as its result.

Here's a simple example of a lambda function that calculates the square of a number:

```
square = lambda x: x ** 2
print(square(5))  # Outputs: 25
```

Lambda functions are particularly useful in the following scenarios:

1. **Short, Simple Functions:** Lambda functions are great for defining short, concise functions that can be written in a single line. This can make your code more readable when the function logic is straightforward.

```
# Using lambda to sort a list of tuples based on the second element of each tuple
data = [(1, 3), (4, 1), (2, 8)]
```

```
sorted_data = sorted(data, key=lambda x: x[1])
```

2. **Functional Programming:** Lambda functions are commonly used in functional programming constructs like **map()**, **filter()**, and **reduce()**. They allow you to define simple operations to be applied to each element of a sequence.

```
# Using lambda with map to double each element of a list
numbers = [1, 2, 3, 4, 5]
doubled_numbers = list(map(lambda x: x * 2, numbers))
```

3. **Callback Functions:** Lambda functions are handy for providing callback functions to higher-order functions or methods. For instance, you can use them to specify custom sorting criteria for a list of objects.

```
# Sorting a list of dictionaries by a specific key using lambda
data = [{'name': 'Alice', 'age': 30}, {'name': 'Bob', 'age': 25}, {'name': 'Charlie', 'age': 35}]
sorted_data = sorted(data, key=lambda x: x['age'])
```

Despite their usefulness in certain contexts, it's essential to use lambda functions judiciously. For more complex logic or functions with multiple expressions or statements, it's generally better to define a regular named function using the **def** keyword for clarity and maintainability. Lambda functions are best suited for simple, one-off operations where brevity and conciseness are valued.

Describe Python's module system and how to create and use modules.

Python's module system is a fundamental feature that allows you to organize code into reusable units. A module is a file containing Python code, including variables, functions, and classes, that can be imported and used in other Python scripts or modules. Python's module system promotes code modularity, reusability, and maintainability.

Here's how to create and use modules in Python:
Creating a Module:

1. **Create a Python File:** To create a module, you start by creating a Python file (with a **.py** extension) containing the code you want to encapsulate. This file can include functions, variables, classes, and executable code.

```
# mymodule.py

def greet(name):
    return f"Hello, {name}!"

def add(a, b):
    return a + b

# Other functions, variables, or classes can be defined here.
```

2. **Module File Naming:** The module's filename should follow Python's naming conventions (letters, numbers, and underscores; no spaces) and end with the **.py** extension.
   Using a Module:
   Once you've created a module, you can use it in other Python scripts or modules by importing it:

```
# Importing the mymodule module
import mymodule

# Using functions from the module
message = mymodule.greet("Alice")
sum_result = mymodule.add(3, 5)

print(message)   # Outputs: 'Hello, Alice!'
print(sum_result) # Outputs: 8
```

You can also use **from** to import specific elements (functions, variables, or classes) from a module:

```
# Importing specific functions from the mymodule module
from mymodule import greet, add

message = greet("Bob")
```

sum_result = add(4, 6)

Using Aliases:

You can assign aliases to modules or imported elements to make them more concise and avoid naming conflicts:

```
# Importing mymodule with an alias
import mymodule as mm

message = mm.greet("Charlie")

# Importing specific function with an alias
from mymodule import add as addition

sum_result = addition(2, 8)
```

Module Search Path:

When you import a module, Python searches for it in specific directories. The search path includes the directory where the current script is located, built-in modules, and directories specified in the **sys.path** list.

Standard Library Modules:

Python comes with a vast standard library containing modules for various tasks, such as working with files, handling regular expressions, and more. You can import these modules just like your custom modules.

```
import os # Importing the os module for working with the operating system
```

Creating Packages:

For more extensive projects, you can organize your modules into packages, which are directories containing multiple related modules and a special **__init__.py** file. This file can be empty or contain initialization code for the package.

```
my_package/
    __init__.py
    module1.py
```

module2.py

To use modules from a package, you import them with the package name:

from my_package import module1

Python's module system is a powerful tool for structuring code, promoting code reuse, and managing project complexity. It allows you to create organized and maintainable codebases by dividing your code into smaller, manageable units that can be developed, tested, and maintained independently.

OBJECT-ORIENTED PROGRAMMING

What is object-oriented programming (OOP) in Python?

Object-Oriented Programming (OOP) is a programming paradigm that focuses on organizing and structuring code using objects. In OOP, an object is a self-contained unit that combines data (attributes) and the operations (methods or functions) that can be performed on that data. Python is an object-oriented programming language that fully supports the principles of OOP.

Here are the core concepts of Object-Oriented Programming in Python:

1. **Objects:** Objects are instances of classes, and they are the fundamental building blocks of OOP in Python. Objects can represent real-world entities, such as a car, a person, or a bank account. Each object has its own unique set of attributes and can perform certain actions (methods).

2. **Classes:** A class is a blueprint or template for creating objects. It defines the structure and behavior that objects of that class will have. Classes encapsulate data (attributes) and functions (methods) that operate on that data. In Python, classes are defined using the **class** keyword.

```
class Car:
    # Class attributes (shared by all instances of the class)
```

```
   make = ""
   model = ""

   # Constructor method to initialize object attributes
   def __init__(self, make, model):
      self.make = make
      self.model = model

   # Method to start the car
   def start(self):
      print(f"{self.make} {self.model} is starting.")
```

3. **Attributes:** Attributes are variables that store data specific to an object. They define the state of an object. In the above example, **make** and **model** are attributes of the **Car** class.

4. **Methods:** Methods are functions defined within a class that operate on the attributes of objects created from that class. They define the behavior of objects. In the **Car** class example, **start()** is a method.

5. **Inheritance:** Inheritance allows you to create a new class (called a subclass or derived class) based on an existing class (called a superclass or base class). The subclass inherits attributes and methods from the superclass and can also add its own attributes and methods. Inheritance promotes code reuse and extensibility.

6. **Polymorphism:** Polymorphism allows objects of different classes to be treated as objects of a common superclass. This enables you to write code that can work with objects of multiple related classes in a consistent way.

7. **Encapsulation:** Encapsulation is the concept of bundling the data (attributes) and the methods that operate on that data into a single unit (a class). It provides data hiding and access control, allowing you to define who can access and modify the data.

8. **Abstraction:** Abstraction is the process of simplifying complex systems by breaking them into smaller, more manageable parts. In OOP, it often involves defining abstract classes or interfaces that provide a high-level view of an object's functionality without getting into the implementation details.

Explain the concepts of classes and objects.

Classes and **objects** are fundamental concepts in Object-Oriented Programming (OOP). They are used to structure and organize code by encapsulating data and behavior.

1. Classes:

- A **class** is a blueprint or template for creating objects. It defines the structure and behavior that objects of that class will have. Classes are like templates that can be used to create multiple instances or objects with similar characteristics.
- In Python, classes are defined using the **class** keyword followed by the class name. The class can contain attributes (variables) and methods (functions) that define the properties and behaviors of objects created from that class.
- Classes encapsulate related data and functions, promoting code modularity and reusability.

Example of a Class:

```python
class Dog:
    # Class attribute
    species = "Canis familiaris"

    # Constructor method to initialize object attributes
    def __init__(self, name, age):
        self.name = name
        self.age = age

    # Method to describe the dog
    def describe(self):
        return f"{self.name} is {self.age} years old."

    # Method to make the dog bark
    def bark(self):
        return "Woof!"
```

2. Objects:

- An **object** is an instance of a class. It is a concrete realization of the class blueprint, with its own unique set of attributes and values.
- Objects represent real-world entities or concepts and can be used

to store data and perform actions (methods).
- Objects are created by calling the class as if it were a function, and the result is an instance of that class.

Example of Objects:

```
# Creating instances (objects) of the Dog class
dog1 = Dog("Buddy", 3)
dog2 = Dog("Molly", 5)


# Accessing object attributes
print(dog1.name)  # Outputs: "Buddy"
print(dog2.age)   # Outputs: 5


# Calling object methods
print(dog1.describe())  # Outputs: "Buddy is 3 years old."
print(dog2.bark())     # Outputs: "Woof!"
```

How do you create and initialize a class in Python?

To create and initialize a class in Python, you follow these steps:
1. **Define the Class:**
   - Use the **class** keyword followed by the class name to define the class. The class name should follow Python's naming conventions (letters, numbers, and underscores; no spaces).
2. **Constructor Method (__init__):**
   - Inside the class, create a special method called **__init__**. This method serves as the constructor and is automatically called when you create a new object from the class.
   - The **__init__** method initializes the attributes of the object. It typically takes at least one argument, which is **self. self** is a reference to the instance of the class and is used to access and modify object attributes.
   - Inside the **__init__** method, initialize the object's attributes by assigning values to them using **self.**
3. **Define Class Attributes and Methods:**
   - Within the class, you can define class attributes (variables shared by all instances of the class) and methods (functions that operate on the object's attributes and perform actions).

Here's an example of creating and initializing a class in Python:

```python
class Dog:
    # Class attribute
    species = "Canis familiaris"

    # Constructor method to initialize object attributes
    def __init__(self, name, age):
        self.name = name
        self.age = age

    # Method to describe the dog
    def describe(self):
        return f"{self.name} is {self.age} years old."

    # Method to make the dog bark
    def bark(self):
        return "Woof!"
```

Now, you can create instances (objects) of the **Dog** class and initialize them with specific attribute values:

```python
# Creating instances (objects) of the Dog class
dog1 = Dog("Buddy", 3)
dog2 = Dog("Molly", 5)
```

In this example, **dog1** and **dog2** are objects created from the **Dog** class. They have their own unique **name** and **age** attributes initialized using the constructor method (**__init__**).

You can access and modify the attributes and call methods on these objects as shown earlier:

```python
print(dog1.name)        # Outputs: "Buddy"
print(dog2.describe())  # Outputs: "Molly is 5 years old."
print(dog1.bark())      # Outputs: "Woof!"
```

By defining classes and initializing objects, you can model real-world entities and encapsulate their data and behavior in a structured and organized manner.

Describe inheritance and its types in Python.

Inheritance is a fundamental concept in Object-Oriented Programming (OOP) that allows you to create a new class based on an existing class. The new class inherits the attributes and methods of the existing class, which is referred to as the **base class** or **superclass**. The new class is called the **derived class** or **subclass**. Inheritance promotes code reuse and the creation of a hierarchy of related classes.

In Python, you can implement inheritance using the **class** definition by specifying the base class in parentheses after the derived class's name. Here's a general syntax:

```
class BaseClass:
    # Base class attributes and methods

class DerivedClass(BaseClass):
    # Derived class attributes and methods
```

Types of Inheritance in Python:
1. **Single Inheritance:**
   - Single inheritance is the simplest form of inheritance where a derived class inherits from a single base class.
   - In this type of inheritance, a subclass can inherit attributes and methods from only one superclass.
   - Example:

```
class Animal:
    def speak(self):
        pass

class Dog(Animal):
    def speak(self):
        return "Woof!"
```

2. **Multiple Inheritance:**
   - Multiple inheritance allows a derived class to inherit from more than one base class.
   - In this type of inheritance, a subclass can inherit attributes and methods from multiple superclasses.

- Example:

```
class Parent1:
    pass

class Parent2:
    pass

class Child(Parent1, Parent2):
    pass
```

3. **Multilevel Inheritance:**
    - Multilevel inheritance involves a chain of inheritance, where a subclass is derived from another subclass.
    - In this type of inheritance, a class acts as both a base class and a derived class.
    - Example:

```
class Grandparent:
    pass

class Parent(Grandparent):
    pass

class Child(Parent):
    pass
```

4. **Hierarchical Inheritance:**
    - Hierarchical inheritance occurs when multiple subclasses inherit from a single base class.
    - In this type of inheritance, multiple classes share a common base class.
    - Example:

```
class Animal:
    pass

class Dog(Animal):
    pass
```

```
class Cat(Animal):
    pass
```

5. **Hybrid Inheritance (Mixing Multiple Types):**
   - Hybrid inheritance is a combination of different types of inheritance, such as single, multiple, and multilevel inheritance.
   - It allows you to create complex class hierarchies to model various relationships in your code.
   - Example:

```
class A:
    pass

class B(A):
    pass

class C(B):
    pass

class D(C, A):
    pass
```

Python's support for inheritance provides flexibility in designing class hierarchies and modeling real-world relationships. When using inheritance, it's important to consider the principles of OOP, such as encapsulation, abstraction, and polymorphism, to create well-structured and maintainable code.

What is method overriding, and how is it implemented in Python?

Method overriding is a concept in Object-Oriented Programming (OOP) that allows a subclass to provide a specific implementation for a method that is already defined in its superclass. When a subclass overrides a method, it provides its own version of the method, which is used when the method is called on objects of the subclass. Method overriding is a way to customize or extend the behavior of a method inherited from a superclass.

In Python, method overriding is implemented as follows:

1. **Define a Superclass (Base Class):**
   - Create a superclass (base class) that contains the method you want to override. This method should be marked as overridable by not including the **@staticmethod** or **@classmethod** decorators.
2. **Create a Subclass (Derived Class):**
   - Create a subclass (derived class) that inherits from the superclass.
3. **Override the Method:**
   - In the subclass, define a method with the same name as the method you want to override. This new method in the subclass should have the same method signature (i.e., the same name and the same parameters) as the method in the superclass.
   - The overridden method in the subclass provides a new implementation specific to the subclass.

Here's an example of method overriding in Python:

```python
class Animal:
    def speak(self):
        return "Animal makes a sound"


class Dog(Animal):
    def speak(self):
        return "Woof!"


class Cat(Animal):
    def speak(self):
        return "Meow!"
```

In this example:
- **Animal** is the superclass with a **speak()** method.
- **Dog** and **Cat** are subclasses that inherit from **Animal**.
- Both **Dog** and **Cat** override the **speak()** method with their own implementations.

Now, to create instances of the **Dog** and **Cat** classes and call the **speak()** method:

```
dog = Dog()
cat = Cat()

print(dog.speak())  # Outputs: "Woof!"
print(cat.speak())  # Outputs: "Meow!"
```

As you can see, when you call the **speak()** method on objects of the **Dog** and **Cat** classes, Python uses the overridden methods in the subclasses to provide custom behavior. Method overriding allows you to specialize the behavior of methods in derived classes while maintaining a consistent interface defined by the superclass.

FILE HANDLING AND INPUT/OUTPUT

How do you open and close files in Python?

In Python, you can open and close files using built-in functions and context managers. Here's how you can do it:

Opening a File:

To open a file, you can use the **open()** function. The **open()** function takes two arguments: the name of the file you want to open and the mode in which you want to open it. Common file modes include:

- **'r'**: Read mode (default). Opens the file for reading.
- **'w'**: Write mode. Opens the file for writing (creates a new file if it doesn't exist or truncates the existing file).
- **'a'**: Append mode. Opens the file for writing (creates a new file if it doesn't exist or appends to the existing file).
- **'b'**: Binary mode. Used in combination with other modes for binary files (e.g., **'rb'** for reading binary).

Here's an example of opening a file in read mode:

```
# Open a file for reading (default mode)
file = open('example.txt', 'r')
```

Closing a File:

After you're done with a file, it's essential to close it to release system resources and ensure that any changes are saved. You can close a file using the **close()** method of the file object:

file.close()

However, manually closing files can be error-prone, especially if exceptions occur while processing the file. To ensure that files are properly closed even in the presence of exceptions, it's recommended to use the **with** statement and context managers.

Using the "with" Statement and Context Managers:
The **with** statement in Python is used in conjunction with context managers to automatically set up and tear down resources. For file handling, it ensures that the file is properly closed when you exit the block of code. You can open and work with a file inside a **with** block:

```python
# Using "with" statement to open and close a file
with open('example.txt', 'r') as file:
    # Perform operations on the file here
    data = file.read()
    print(data)

# The file is automatically closed when the block exits
```

Using the **with** statement is considered a best practice for file handling in Python because it ensures proper resource management and eliminates the need for explicit **file.close()** calls.

Explain the different modes for opening files.

In Python, you can open files in different modes, depending on how you intend to interact with the file. These modes determine whether the file will be read, written to, or both. Here are the most common file modes:

1. **Read Mode ('r'):**
   - Mode: **'r'**
   - Description: Opens the file for reading (default mode).
   - Use Cases: Reading the contents of an existing file.
   - Behavior:
     - If the file does not exist, it raises a **FileNotFoundError**.

- Reading operations (**read()**, **readline()**, **readlines()**) are allowed.
- Writing operations are not allowed.

```
with open('example.txt', 'r') as file:
   data = file.read()
```

2. **Write Mode ('w')**:
   - Mode: **'w'**
   - Description: Opens the file for writing (creates a new file or truncates an existing one).
   - Use Cases: Creating a new file or overwriting an existing file.
- Behavior:
     - If the file exists, it is truncated (emptied). If it doesn't exist, a new empty file is created.
     - Writing operations (**write()**, **writelines()**) are allowed.
   - Reading operations are not allowed.

```
with open('example.txt', 'w') as file:
   file.write('Hello, World!')
```

3. **Append Mode ('a')**:
   - Mode: **'a'**
   - Description: Opens the file for writing (creates a new file or appends to an existing one).
   - Use Cases: Appending data to an existing file.
- Behavior:
     - If the file exists, the data is appended to the end of the file. If it doesn't exist, a new empty file is created.
     - Writing operations are allowed.
   - Reading operations are not allowed.

```
with open('example.txt', 'a') as file:
   file.write(' Appended text.')
```

4. **Binary Mode ('b')**:
   - Mode: **'b'** (e.g., **'rb'**, **'wb'**)
   - Description: Used in combination with other modes for

binary files.
- Use Cases: Reading or writing binary data, such as images or binary formats.
- Behavior:
    - When used, the file is treated as a binary file, and data is read/written in binary format.
    - Commonly used with modes **'rb'** (read binary) and **'wb'** (write binary).

```
with open('binary_data.bin', 'rb') as file:
    binary_data = file.read()
```

5. **Text Mode ('t')**:
   - Mode: **'t'** (e.g., **'rt'**, **'wt'**)
   - Description: Used in combination with other modes for text files (default for read mode).
   - Use Cases: Reading or writing text data (characters, strings).
- Behavior:
    - When used, the file is treated as a text file, and data is read/written as text (strings).
    - Commonly used with modes **'rt'** (read text) and **'wt'** (write text).

```
with open('text_data.txt', 'rt') as file:
    text = file.read()
```

These are the primary modes for opening files in Python. You can combine text and binary modes with read, write, or append modes to suit your specific file handling needs. Always ensure that you choose the appropriate mode based on whether you intend to read, write, or both, and be cautious when using write modes to prevent unintentional data loss.

What is the purpose of the "with" statement in file handling?

The **with** statement in Python is used for **context management** and is particularly valuable in file handling. It is designed to simplify the management of external resources, such as files, network connections, or database connections, by ensuring that the necessary setup and cleanup actions are performed reliably, even in the presence of exceptions or errors.

In the context of file handling, the primary purpose of the **with** statement is to:

1. **Automatically Open Files:** The **with** statement automatically opens the file specified and creates a file object for you to work with. You specify the file name and the file mode as arguments to the **open()** function within the **with** statement.
2. **Automatic Closing of Files:** When the code block under the **with** statement exits (either normally or due to an exception), the file is automatically closed. This ensures that resources are released, and any pending writes are flushed to the file.

The **with** statement follows this general structure:

```
with open('file.txt', 'mode') as file:
    # Code block for working with the file
```

Here's why the **with** statement is essential in file handling:

1. Resource Management: It guarantees that the file is properly closed when you're done with it. This is crucial for freeing up system resources, ensuring data integrity, and avoiding potential file corruption.

2. Error Handling: If an exception occurs while working with the file, the **with** statement ensures that the file is still closed, preventing data loss and resource leaks. It promotes robust error handling.

3. Cleaner Code: The **with** statement results in more concise and readable code because you don't need to explicitly open and close the file using **file.open()** and **file.close()** methods. The context manager handles these details.

Example:

```
with open('example.txt', 'r') as file:
    data = file.read()
    # Do operations with the file
# File is automatically closed here, even if an exception occurs
```

How do you read and write text files in Python?

In Python, you can read and write text files using the built-in **open()** function and various file methods. Here's how you can perform these operations:

Reading Text Files:

To read the contents of a text file, you can follow these steps:

1. **Open the File in Read Mode ('r'):**
   - Use the **open()** function to open the file in read mode (**'r'**).
   - Provide the file's path and name as the first argument and specify the mode as **'r'**.
2. **Read the File Contents:**
   - Use the **read()** method of the file object to read the entire file contents into a string.
   - Alternatively, you can use **readline()** to read one line at a time or **readlines()** to read all lines into a list.
3. **Close the File:**
   - Ensure that you close the file using the **close()** method of the file object to release system resources.

Here's an example of reading a text file:

```
# Open the file in read mode
with open('example.txt', 'r') as file:
    # Read the entire file into a string
    data = file.read()


# File is automatically closed when the "with" block exits
```

Writing to Text Files:

To write data to a text file, you can follow these steps:

1. **Open the File in Write Mode ('w'):**
   - Use the **open()** function to open the file in write mode (**'w'**).
   - Provide the file's path and name as the first argument and specify the mode as **'w'**.
2. **Write Data to the File:**
   - Use the **write()** method of the file object to write data to the file. This method takes a string as its argument.
3. **Close the File:**
   - Ensure that you close the file using the **close()** method of the file object to save the changes and release resources.

Here's an example of writing to a text file:

```
# Open the file in write mode
with open('example.txt', 'w') as file:
    # Write data to the file
    file.write('Hello, World!')
```

```
# File is automatically closed when the "with" block exits
```

Appending to Text Files:
If you want to add new data to an existing text file without overwriting its contents, you can use append mode (**'a'**). The process is similar to writing, but you open the file in append mode (**'a'**) instead of write mode (**'w'**).

Here's an example of appending to a text file:

```
# Open the file in append mode
with open('example.txt', 'a') as file:
    # Append data to the file
    file.write('\nAppended text.')
```

```
# File is automatically closed when the "with" block exits
```

By following these steps, you can effectively read and write text files in Python while ensuring proper resource management and data integrity.

Describe binary file handling in Python.

Binary file handling in Python involves reading and writing files in their binary representation, which means dealing with data at the byte level rather than as text or character data. Binary files can contain any type of data, including images, audio, video, executables, and more. To handle binary files in Python, you use modes like **'rb'** for reading binary and **'wb'** for writing binary.

Here's how to work with binary files in Python:

Reading Binary Files:
1. **Open the Binary File in Read Mode ('rb'):**
   - Use the **open()** function to open the binary file in read mode (**'rb'**).

- Provide the file's path and name as the first argument and specify the mode as **'rb'**.

2. **Read Data from the File:**
   - Use the **read()** method of the file object to read binary data from the file.
   - The **read()** method returns the data as bytes.

3. **Close the File:**
   - Always close the file using the **close()** method of the file object when you're done reading.

Here's an example of reading a binary file:

```
# Open the binary file in read mode
with open('image.jpg', 'rb') as file:
    # Read binary data from the file
    binary_data = file.read()

# File is automatically closed when the "with" block exits
```

Writing to Binary Files:

1. **Open the Binary File in Write Mode ('wb'):**
   - Use the **open()** function to open the binary file in write mode ('wb').
   - Provide the file's path and name as the first argument and specify the mode as **'wb'**.

2. **Write Data to the File:**
   - Use the **write()** method of the file object to write binary data to the file.
   - Provide the data as bytes.

3. **Close the File:**
   - Make sure to close the file using the **close()** method of the file object to save the changes and release resources.

Here's an example of writing to a binary file:

```
# Binary data to write
binary_data                                          = b'\x48\x65\x6C\x6C\x6F\x2C\x20\x57\x6F\x72\x6C\x64\x21'

# Open the binary file in write mode
with open('binary_data.bin', 'wb') as file:
```

```
# Write binary data to the file
file.write(binary_data)
```

```
# File is automatically closed when the "with" block exits
```

Working with binary files gives you the flexibility to handle various types of data, including non-textual and non-human-readable data. It's essential to understand the binary representation of your data and ensure that you read and write it correctly.

DATA STRUCTURES

What are the built-in data structures in Python?

Python provides several built-in data structures that serve various purposes. These data structures are essential for organizing and manipulating data efficiently. The primary built-in data structures in Python include:

1. **Lists (list):**
   - Lists are ordered collections of items.
   - They can contain elements of different data types.
   - Lists are mutable, which means you can change their contents (add, remove, or modify elements).

2. **Tuples (tuple):**
   - Tuples are similar to lists but are immutable, meaning their contents cannot be changed once they are created.
   - They are often used to represent fixed collections of elements.

3. **Dictionaries (dict):**
   - Dictionaries are collections of key-value pairs.
   - They are unordered and allow you to access values by their associated keys.
   - Dictionaries are highly efficient for data retrieval.

4. **Sets (set) and Frozensets (frozenset):**
   - Sets are collections of unique elements with no specific order.
   - Frozensets are immutable sets.

- Sets are useful for tasks requiring membership testing and eliminating duplicates.

5. **Strings (str):**
   - Strings are sequences of characters.
   - They are immutable, meaning you cannot modify individual characters in a string.

6. **Bytes and Byte Arrays (bytes, bytearray):**
   - Bytes and byte arrays are used to represent binary data.
   - Bytes are immutable, while byte arrays are mutable.

7. **Stacks and Queues (Using Lists):**
   - Stacks and queues are abstract data types.
   - Stacks follow the Last-In-First-Out (LIFO) principle.
   - Queues follow the First-In-First-Out (FIFO) principle.
   - They can be implemented using lists or collections.deque.

8. **Linked Lists:**
   - Linked lists are a dynamic data structure composed of nodes.
   - They consist of a head node and each node points to the next node in the sequence.
   - Python does not have a built-in linked list type, but you can implement one using classes.

9. **Trees:**
   - Trees are hierarchical data structures consisting of nodes.
   - They include binary trees, binary search trees, and more.
   - Trees are often used for representing hierarchical data.

10. **Graphs:**
    - Graphs are used to represent relationships between entities.
    - They can be directed or undirected and contain nodes and edges.
    - Python does not have a built-in graph type, but you can implement graphs using custom classes or external libraries.

11. **Dictionaries (collections module):**
    - The **collections** module provides specialized dictionary types like **defaultdict** and **OrderedDict** with additional functionalities.

12. **Heaps (heapq module):**
    - The **heapq** module offers heap-related operations for lists, allowing you to create min-heaps and max-heaps.

13. **Hash Tables (hashlib module):**
    - The **hashlib** module provides various hash functions and is

used for hashing data.
14. **Deques (collections module):**
   - Deques (double-ended queues) are efficient for adding and removing elements from both ends.
   - They are available in the **collections** module.
15. **Named Tuples (collections module):**
   - Named tuples are similar to regular tuples but have named fields for improved readability and self-documentation.

These built-in data structures, along with Python's extensive standard library, provide powerful tools for solving a wide range of programming problems. Choosing the right data structure for your specific task is crucial for writing efficient and maintainable code.

Explain the difference between lists and tuples.

Lists and **tuples** are both fundamental data structures in Python, but they have some key differences:

1. **Mutability:**
   - **Lists:** Lists are **mutable**, which means you can change their contents after creation. You can add, remove, or modify elements in a list.
   - **Tuples:** Tuples, on the other hand, are **immutable**, meaning their contents cannot be changed once they are created. Once you define a tuple, you cannot add, remove, or modify elements.

Example of a list:

```
my_list = [1, 2, 3]
my_list.append(4)  # This is allowed
my_list[0] = 0     # This is allowed
```

Example of a tuple:

```
my_tuple = (1, 2, 3)
# The following operations are not allowed and will result in an error:
# my_tuple.append(4)
# my_tuple[0] = 0
```

2. **Syntax:**

- **Lists:** Lists are defined using square brackets [ ].
- **Tuples:** Tuples are defined using parentheses ( ). Optionally, you can include a comma after the elements, even for single-element tuples, to distinguish them from expressions enclosed in regular parentheses.

```
my_list = [1, 2, 3]
my_tuple = (1, 2, 3)  # or my_tuple = 1, 2, 3 (with or without parentheses)
```

3. **Performance:**
   - **Lists:** Lists, being mutable, can incur slightly more memory and processing overhead compared to tuples because they need to support operations that modify the list.
   - **Tuples:** Tuples, being immutable, are generally more memory-efficient and can have faster access times compared to lists. They are a good choice for storing data that should not change during program execution.
4. **Use Cases:**
   - **Lists:** Lists are suitable for collections of items where the order and content may change over time. They are commonly used for dynamic collections, such as lists of items to process or manipulate.
   - **Tuples:** Tuples are often used to represent fixed collections of items that should not be modified. They are suitable for cases where you want to ensure data integrity and immutability, such as coordinates, configurations, or function return values.
5. **Iteration:**
   - Both lists and tuples support iteration using **for** loops and can be used interchangeably in most iteration scenarios.

How do you work with dictionaries in Python?

Working with dictionaries in Python involves creating, accessing, modifying, and manipulating key-value pairs. Dictionaries are unordered collections of data where each element is stored as a key-value pair. Here are the fundamental operations for working with dictionaries:

Creating a Dictionary:

You can create a dictionary by enclosing a comma-separated list of key-value pairs within curly braces **{}** or by using the **dict()** constructor.

```
# Creating a dictionary using curly braces
my_dict = {'name': 'John', 'age': 30, 'city': 'New York'}

# Creating a dictionary using the dict() constructor
another_dict = dict(name='Alice', age=25, city='San Francisco')
```

Accessing Values:
You can access the values in a dictionary by specifying the key in square brackets **[]** or by using the **get()** method.

```
name = my_dict['name']  # Accessing 'name' value
age = my_dict.get('age')   # Using get() method to access 'age' value
```

Modifying Values:
You can change the value associated with a key in a dictionary by assigning a new value to that key.

```
my_dict['age'] = 31 # Modifying the 'age' value
```

Adding New Key-Value Pairs:
To add a new key-value pair to a dictionary, simply assign a value to a new key.

```
my_dict['city'] = 'Los Angeles' # Adding a new key-value pair
```

Removing Key-Value Pairs:
You can remove a key-value pair from a dictionary using the **del** statement or the **pop()** method.

```
del my_dict['city']  # Removing the 'city' key-value pair
age = my_dict.pop('age')  # Removing and getting the 'age' value
```

Iterating Through a Dictionary:
You can loop through the keys, values, or key-value pairs in a

dictionary using **for** loops.

```
# Iterating through keys
for key in my_dict:
    print(key)

# Iterating through values
for value in my_dict.values():
    print(value)

# Iterating through key-value pairs
for key, value in my_dict.items():
    print(key, value)
```

Checking for Key Existence:
You can check if a key exists in a dictionary using the **in** keyword or the **get()** method.

```
if 'age' in my_dict:
    print("Age is present in the dictionary")

value = my_dict.get('name', 'Unknown')   # Using get() with a default value
```

Dictionary Methods:
Python dictionaries have several built-in methods for various operations, including **keys()**, **values()**, **items()**, **update()**, **clear()**, and **copy()**.

```
keys = my_dict.keys()  # Get a list of keys
values = my_dict.values()  # Get a list of values
items = my_dict.items()  # Get a list of key-value pairs
my_dict.update({'country': 'USA'})   # Add multiple key-value pairs
my_dict.clear()  # Remove all key-value pairs
copy_dict = my_dict.copy()   # Create a shallow copy of the dictionary
```

Dictionaries are versatile data structures used for tasks like data storage, configuration management, and data retrieval. They are particularly efficient when you need to look up values based on specific keys. Understanding how to work with dictionaries is essential for many Python programming tasks.

Describe sets and their use cases.

Sets in Python are unordered collections of unique elements. Unlike lists or tuples, where elements can be repeated and have a specific order, sets only contain distinct elements, and their order is not guaranteed. Sets are implemented using a hash table, which makes membership tests (checking if an element is in a set) highly efficient.

Here are the key characteristics and use cases for sets in Python:

Characteristics of Sets:

1. **Uniqueness:** Sets only store unique elements. If you try to add a duplicate element to a set, it won't be added.

2. **Unordered:** Sets are unordered collections, meaning the elements do not have a specific order. The order in which elements were added may not be preserved.

3. **Mutable:** Sets are mutable, so you can add or remove elements after creation.

Creating Sets:

You can create sets in Python using curly braces **{}** or the **set()** constructor.

```
my_set = {1, 2, 3}  # Using curly braces
another_set = set([3, 4, 5])  # Using set() constructor with a list
```

Adding and Removing Elements:

To add elements to a set, you can use the **add()** method. To remove elements, you can use the **remove()** method. If you want to avoid raising an error when removing an element that doesn't exist, you can use the **discard()** method.

```
my_set.add(4)  # Adding an element
my_set.remove(2)  # Removing an element
my_set.discard(10)   # Removing an element without raising an error if it doesn't exist
```

Set Operations:

Sets support various set operations, such as union, intersection, difference, and symmetric difference, which can be performed using built-in methods or operators (**|**, **&**, **-**, **^**).

```
set1 = {1, 2, 3}
set2 = {3, 4, 5}

union_set = set1 | set2  # Union
intersection_set = set1 & set2  # Intersection
difference_set = set1 - set2  # Difference
symmetric_difference_set = set1 ^ set2  # Symmetric Difference
```

Checking Membership:

You can efficiently check whether an element is in a set using the **in** operator.

```
if 3 in my_set:
    print("3 is in the set")
```

Use Cases for Sets:

Sets are handy in various programming scenarios, including:

1. **Removing Duplicates:** Use sets to remove duplicate elements from a list or other collection. By converting the collection to a set and back to a list, you retain the unique elements.
2. **Membership Testing:** Sets are ideal for efficiently testing whether an element is present in a collection.
3. **Mathematical Set Operations:** Sets are valuable for performing mathematical set operations like union, intersection, and difference, often used in data analysis and processing.
4. **Counting Unique Items:** Sets can be used to count the number of unique items in a collection.
5. **Configuration Management:** Sets can be used to store and manage configuration options, ensuring that each option is unique.
6. **Network or Graph Algorithms:** Sets are useful in graph algorithms like finding connected components or checking node existence.
7. **Filtering Data:** Sets can be used to filter data based on specific

criteria, such as filtering out irrelevant data points.

What is the difference between shallow and deep copying of data structures?

Shallow copying and deep copying are two methods for duplicating data structures, such as lists or dictionaries, in Python. The main difference between them lies in how they handle nested objects (objects within objects).

Shallow Copy:

- A shallow copy of a data structure creates a new object (e.g., list or dictionary) but does not create copies of the objects contained within the original data structure. Instead, it references the same objects as the original data structure.
- Shallow copying is performed using methods like **copy.copy()** for general objects, **list.copy()** for lists, and **dict.copy()** for dictionaries.
- Changes made to objects within the copied data structure will be reflected in the original data structure and vice versa if those objects are mutable.
- Shallow copies are generally faster and consume less memory since they don't duplicate nested objects.

Here's an example of shallow copying:

```
import copy

original_list = [1, [2, 3]]
shallow_copied_list = copy.copy(original_list)

# Modifying the nested list in the shallow copy
shallow_copied_list[1][0] = 99

print(original_list)        # Output: [1, [99, 3]]
print(shallow_copied_list)   # Output: [1, [99, 3]]
```

In the example above, the change made to the nested list within **shallow_copied_list** is also reflected in the **original_list**.

Deep Copy:

- A deep copy of a data structure creates a completely independent duplicate of the data structure and all the objects contained within it, recursively.

- Deep copying is performed using the **copy.deepcopy()** function from the **copy** module.
- Changes made to objects within the copied data structure will not affect the original data structure, even for mutable objects.
- Deep copies are generally slower and consume more memory since they recursively duplicate all objects within the data structure.

Here's an example of deep copying:

```
import copy

original_list = [1, [2, 3]]
deep_copied_list = copy.deepcopy(original_list)

# Modifying the nested list in the deep copy
deep_copied_list[1][0] = 99

print(original_list)        # Output: [1, [2, 3]]
print(deep_copied_list)    # Output: [1, [99, 3]]
```

In the example above, the change made to the nested list within **deep_copied_list** does not affect the **original_list**.

Choosing Between Shallow and Deep Copy:

- Use shallow copying when you want a new data structure that shares references to nested objects with the original. This can be useful for certain scenarios to save memory and speed.
- Use deep copying when you need a completely independent copy of the data structure and its nested objects, ensuring that changes to one do not affect the other.

The choice between shallow and deep copying depends on your specific use case and whether you want changes to one copy to propagate to the other or remain independent.

EXCEPTION HANDLING AND DEBUGGING

How does Python handle exceptions?

Python handles exceptions using a mechanism that allows you to gracefully respond to errors during program execution. This mechanism involves the use of **try**, **except**, **else**, and **finally** blocks. Here's how Python handles exceptions:

1. **Error Occurs:** When an error (an exception) occurs during program execution, Python raises an exception. An exception is a Python object that represents an error condition.

2. **Exception Handling with try and except Blocks:**
   - To handle exceptions, you enclose the potentially problematic code inside a **try** block.
   - You then specify one or more **except** blocks to catch and handle specific exceptions. Each **except** block can handle a particular type of exception or a group of related exceptions.
   - If an exception occurs within the **try** block that matches one of the **except** blocks, Python transfers control to the corresponding **except** block.
   - You can have multiple **except** blocks to handle different types of exceptions.

```
try:
```

```
    # Code that may raise an exception
    result = 10 / 0  # This raises a ZeroDivisionError
except ZeroDivisionError:
    # Handle the ZeroDivisionError
    result = float('inf')  # Assign a safe value
except Exception as e:
    # Handle other exceptions
    print(f"An error occurred: {e}")
```

3. **The else Block:**
    - You can include an optional **else** block immediately after the **try** and **except** blocks.
    - Code within the **else** block executes if no exceptions are raised within the **try** block.
  - It's typically used for code that should run only when no exceptions occur.

```
try:
    result = 10 / 2  # This is safe, no exception will be raised
except ZeroDivisionError:
    print("Division by zero error")
else:
    print(f"Result is {result}")  # This will execute
```

4. **The finally Block:**
    - You can include an optional **finally** block after the **try**, **except**, and **else** blocks.
    - Code within the **finally** block executes regardless of whether an exception was raised or not.
  - It's often used for cleanup tasks, such as closing files or releasing resources.

```
try:
    file = open('example.txt', 'r')
    # Code that may raise an exception
except FileNotFoundError:
    print("File not found")
finally:
    file.close()  # Ensure the file is closed, even if an exception
```

occurred

5. **Propagation of Unhandled Exceptions:**
   - If an exception is raised and not caught by any **except** block in the current function, it propagates up the call stack to higher-level functions.
   - If the exception propagates all the way up to the top-level of your program and is still not caught, the program terminates, and an error message is displayed.

Python's exception handling mechanism allows you to gracefully handle errors, preventing program crashes and providing informative error messages. By catching and handling exceptions, you can take appropriate actions to recover from errors or terminate the program gracefully, improving the overall reliability of your software.

What is the purpose of "raise" in exception handling?

The **raise** statement in Python is used to explicitly raise an exception or error within your code. It allows you to signal that a specific exceptional condition has occurred during the execution of your program. Here are the primary purposes of the **raise** statement in exception handling:

1. **Signaling Errors:** You can use **raise** to signal that a particular error or exceptional condition has occurred in your code. This is particularly useful when you encounter a situation that is not automatically detected by Python's built-in exception handling mechanisms.

   pythonCopy code

   if some_condition: raise ValueError("This is a custom error message")

   In this example, if **some_condition** evaluates to **True**, it raises a **ValueError** exception with the specified error message.

2. **Custom Exceptions:** You can define your own custom exceptions by creating a new class that inherits from the built-in **Exception** class or one of its subclasses. This allows you to create exception types tailored to your application's specific needs.

   pythonCopy code

class MyCustomError(Exception): pass def my_function(): if some_condition: raise MyCustomError("Something went wrong in my_function")

In this case, **MyCustomError** is a custom exception that you can raise when specific conditions warrant it.

3. **Handling Special Cases:** You can use **raise** to handle exceptional cases or edge cases that require different error handling logic than the default behavior provided by Python's built-in exceptions.

pythonCopy code

try: result = perform_operation() except SomeError: # Handle the general error case except SpecificError: # Handle a specific error except Exception as e: if special_case: raise SomeOtherError("Special case error: " + str(e)) else: raise

In this example, **raise** is used within an **except** block to raise a different exception (**SomeOtherError**) under a special condition while still allowing other exceptions to propagate.

4. **Error Logging and Debugging:** When an error occurs in your program, you can use **raise** to capture relevant information and log it before re-raising the exception. This can be helpful for debugging and troubleshooting.

pythonCopy code

try: result = perform_operation() except SomeError as e: log_error(e) raise

Here, the **log_error()** function captures information about the error before re-raising it for further handling or reporting.

Explain the importance of debugging in Python.

Debugging is a crucial aspect of software development in Python (and programming in general). It plays a pivotal role in ensuring the reliability, correctness, and maintainability of your Python programs. Here's why debugging is so important:

1. **Identifying and Resolving Errors:**
   * Debugging helps you find and fix errors or bugs in your code. These errors can be syntax errors, runtime errors (exceptions), logical errors, or other issues that prevent your

program from working correctly.

- Early identification and resolution of errors save time and prevent issues from propagating into the production environment.

2. **Ensuring Program Reliability:**
   - Debugging ensures that your Python programs run reliably. It helps you eliminate unexpected crashes, freezes, or unexpected behavior, which can lead to loss of data or damage to your application's reputation.

3. **Improving Code Quality:**
   - Debugging is an essential part of code quality assurance. It helps you maintain high code standards and ensures that your code is clean, readable, and well-structured.
   - Debugging also aids in identifying and eliminating code smells, such as redundant code, unnecessary complexity, and poorly organized code.

4. **Enhancing User Experience:**
   - Debugging contributes to a better user experience. By identifying and fixing issues, you can provide users with software that works as expected, leading to higher user satisfaction and retention.

5. **Efficient Use of Resources:**
   - Debugging helps you optimize your code and improve resource utilization. Identifying and resolving performance bottlenecks or memory leaks ensures that your Python programs run efficiently.

6. **Facilitating Collaboration:**
   - When working in teams, debugging allows team members to understand and fix each other's code. It promotes collaboration and knowledge sharing, making the development process smoother and more productive.

7. **Preventing Security Vulnerabilities:**
   - Debugging helps identify security vulnerabilities and weaknesses in your code. By addressing these issues, you can protect your application from potential threats and attacks.

8. **Supporting Long-Term Maintenance:**
   - As software evolves, debugging becomes crucial for maintaining and updating the codebase. It helps you adapt your code to changing requirements and technologies.

9. **Continuous Improvement:**
   - Debugging is an ongoing process that encourages continuous improvement. By reviewing and analyzing the errors you encounter, you can learn from your mistakes and become a more proficient programmer.
10. **Enhancing Problem-Solving Skills:**
    - Debugging challenges your problem-solving skills and critical thinking. It allows you to develop a deeper understanding of your code and the underlying concepts.
11. **Optimizing Development Time:**
    - Effective debugging reduces the time spent on manual code inspection and guesswork. This optimization streamlines the development process and accelerates project timelines.

What tools are available for debugging Python code?

Debugging Python code is made easier and more efficient with the help of various debugging tools and techniques. Here are some commonly used tools and approaches for debugging Python code:

1. **Print Statements:**
   - The simplest form of debugging involves adding **print** statements to your code to output variable values, messages, or markers at specific points.
   - Example:

```python
print("Reached this point")
print("Variable x:", x)
```

2. **Debugger in Integrated Development Environments (IDEs):**
   - Many Python IDEs, such as PyCharm, Visual Studio Code, and PyDev for Eclipse, come with built-in debugging tools.
   - These tools allow you to set breakpoints, step through code, inspect variables, and watch expressions.
   - You can start debugging sessions directly from your IDE.
3. **pdb (Python Debugger):**
   - **pdb** is the built-in Python debugger that can be used from the command line.

- You can insert **pdb** into your code by adding the following line where you want to start debugging:

import pdb; pdb.set_trace()

- This opens an interactive debugger session when the code is executed.

4. **IPython Debugger (%debug magic command):**
   - IPython, an interactive Python shell, provides a powerful debugger accessible using the **%debug** magic command.
   - You can invoke it in IPython by running **%debug** after an error has occurred to examine the stack trace and variables.

5. **breakpoint() Function (Python 3.7+):**
   - Python 3.7 introduced the **breakpoint()** function, which can be used for debugging.
   - You can insert it into your code where you want to set a breakpoint.
   - When executed, it enters the debugger, allowing you to inspect the program state.

6. **Logging (logging module):**
   - The **logging** module in Python allows you to log messages and information at various levels (e.g., debug, info, error).
   - You can use logging to record program events and errors, which is helpful for debugging and monitoring.

7. **Third-Party Debugging Libraries:**
   - Several third-party libraries offer enhanced debugging features, such as **pudb**, **pdb++**, and **pdbpp**. These provide more advanced debugging capabilities compared to the standard **pdb**.

8. **PySnooper:**
   - PySnooper is a library that helps you quickly debug your code by adding a decorator to functions or blocks of code.
   - It logs variable values and execution flow without cluttering your code with print statements.

9. **Visual Debugging Tools:**
   - Some visual debugging tools, like Winpdb and PyCharm's visual debugger, provide a graphical interface for debugging Python code.

10. **Unit Testing and Test Runners:**

- Using unit tests and test runners like **unittest** and **pytest** can help identify and isolate issues in your code by systematically testing individual components.

11. **Profiling Tools:**
    - Profiling tools like **cProfile** and **line_profiler** help you analyze code performance and identify bottlenecks that may not be apparent during regular debugging.

12. **Code Linters and Static Analyzers:**
    - Tools like **pylint, flake8**, and **mypy** can help detect code style issues and type-related errors before runtime, reducing the need for debugging.

13. **Remote Debugging:**
    - Some tools and IDEs support remote debugging, allowing you to debug code running on remote servers or embedded systems.

14. **Memory Debugging Tools:**
    - Tools like **memory_profiler** help you identify memory leaks and inefficient memory usage in your Python code.

Selecting the appropriate debugging tool depends on your specific needs and preferences. The choice may also vary depending on whether you prefer command-line debugging, IDE-based debugging, or other approaches. Combining multiple tools and techniques can provide comprehensive coverage for debugging Python code effectively.

How do you handle common debugging scenarios?

Debugging is an essential skill in programming, and handling common debugging scenarios effectively can save you a lot of time and frustration. Here's how to approach some common debugging scenarios in Python:

1. **Syntax Errors:**
    - **Issue:** You encounter a syntax error when running your code, and Python raises a **SyntaxError** with an error message indicating the problem.
    - **Handling:** Carefully review the error message, starting with the line and character where the error occurred. Common syntax errors include missing colons, unmatched parentheses,

and misspelled keywords. Correct the syntax error based on the error message's guidance.

2. **Runtime Errors (Exceptions):**
   - **Issue:** Your code raises a runtime exception (e.g., **ZeroDivisionError**, **NameError**, **TypeError**) during execution.

- **Handling:**
  - Use a **try** and **except** block to catch and handle the exception gracefully.
  - Print or log the exception details to understand the cause.
  - Inspect the traceback to identify the line and context of the error.
  - Consider adding informative error messages to your exceptions.
  - Test edge cases and boundary conditions to catch potential exceptions early.

3. **Infinite Loops or Long-Running Code:**
   - **Issue:** Your code seems to be stuck in an infinite loop or takes longer to execute than expected.

- **Handling:**
  - Interrupt the program (e.g., press **Ctrl+C** in the terminal) to stop it.
  - Review the loop conditions or recursive calls to identify the cause of the infinite loop.
  - Use profiling tools like **cProfile** to analyze code performance.
  - Set timeouts or limits for long-running code to prevent infinite waits.

4. **Value or Output Verification:**
   - **Issue:** Your code produces unexpected output or incorrect results.

- **Handling:**
  - Add **print** statements to display intermediate values and variables.
  - Use assertions to verify that specific conditions hold true at various points in your code.
  - Compare your results with expected outcomes and use test cases to verify correctness.

5. **Memory Issues (Memory Leaks or High Usage):**
   - **Issue:** Your program consumes excessive memory or exhibits memory leaks, causing performance issues.
- **Handling:**
     - Use memory profiling tools like **memory_profiler** to identify memory-hungry parts of your code.
     - Review your data structures and ensure efficient memory usage.
     - Explicitly release resources (e.g., close files, disconnect from databases) when they are no longer needed.
   - Consider using garbage collection techniques and tools like **gc** module.
6. **Multithreading or Multiprocessing Issues:**
   - **Issue:** Your code uses multithreading or multiprocessing and encounters issues like race conditions or deadlocks.
- **Handling:**
     - Review your threading/multiprocessing code for shared resources and proper synchronization mechanisms (e.g., locks, semaphores).
     - Use debugging tools like **threading** and **multiprocessing** modules to inspect thread or process states.
   - Be cautious when using global variables shared between threads or processes.
7. **Library or Third-Party Module Integration:**
   - **Issue:** You are encountering errors or unexpected behavior when using external libraries or modules.
- **Handling:**
     - Check the library's documentation and examples for proper usage.
     - Verify that you are using the correct version of the library.
     - Ensure that required dependencies are installed.
   - If the issue persists, consult the library's community or support resources.
8. **Complex Logical Errors:**
   - **Issue:** Your code has logical errors that are not apparent from error messages or exceptions.

- **Handling:**
  - Break down your code into smaller, testable units (functions or methods).
  - Isolate the specific part of the code causing the issue.
  - Use debugging tools like print statements, breakpoints, and step-by-step debugging in IDEs to inspect variables and control flow.
  - Consider reviewing your algorithm and logic, discussing the problem with colleagues, or seeking external feedback.

9. **Integration Testing and Edge Cases:**
  - **Issue:** Your code works fine in normal scenarios but fails in edge cases or specific integration scenarios.

- **Handling:**
  - Develop comprehensive test cases that cover a wide range of scenarios, including edge cases.
  - Use testing frameworks like **unittest** or **pytest** to automate testing.
  - Monitor and log test results and failures to pinpoint integration issues.

10. **Continuous Improvement:**
  - **Handling:** Embrace a continuous improvement mindset by learning from debugging experiences. Document common issues and solutions to build a knowledge base.
  - Conduct code reviews and seek feedback from peers to catch potential issues early.

- Explore best practices, design patterns, and code quality tools to prevent future bugs.

PYTHON LIBRARIES AND FRAMEWORKS

What are the popular libraries for data manipulation in Python?

Python offers several popular libraries for data manipulation, making it a go-to language for data scientists and analysts. These libraries provide powerful tools for cleaning, transforming, and analyzing data. Here are some of the most widely used libraries for data manipulation in Python:

1. **pandas:**
   - **Key Features:** pandas is one of the most essential data manipulation libraries in Python. It provides data structures like DataFrames and Series, along with a wide range of functions for data cleaning, filtering, aggregation, merging, and more. It excels in handling tabular data.
   - **Use Cases:** Data cleaning, data exploration, data preprocessing, data transformation, and basic analysis.
2. **NumPy (Numerical Python):**
   - **Key Features:** NumPy is the fundamental library for numerical computing in Python. It introduces the **ndarray** data structure for efficient handling of arrays and matrices, enabling fast mathematical operations and element-wise array operations.
   - **Use Cases:** Numeric computing, scientific computing, linear algebra, statistical analysis.

3. **SciPy (Scientific Python):**
   - **Key Features:** SciPy builds on NumPy and offers additional functionality for scientific and technical computing. It includes modules for optimization, integration, interpolation, signal and image processing, and more.
   - **Use Cases:** Scientific computing, optimization, integration, signal processing, image processing.
4. **Matplotlib:**
   - **Key Features:** Matplotlib is a versatile library for creating static, animated, and interactive visualizations. It provides a MATLAB-like interface for plotting graphs, charts, and other data visualizations.
   - **Use Cases:** Data visualization, charting, plotting, creating graphs.
5. **Seaborn:**
   - **Key Features:** Seaborn is built on top of Matplotlib and offers a higher-level interface for creating aesthetically pleasing statistical visualizations. It simplifies the creation of complex plots and provides support for statistical estimation.
   - **Use Cases:** Statistical data visualization, data exploration, exploratory data analysis (EDA).
6. **Plotly:**
   - **Key Features:** Plotly is an interactive graphing library that allows you to create interactive, web-based visualizations and dashboards. It supports a wide range of chart types and is often used for data presentation.
   - **Use Cases:** Interactive data visualization, web-based dashboards, data storytelling.
7. **Bokeh:**
   - **Key Features:** Bokeh is another interactive visualization library that specializes in creating interactive, browser-based plots and applications. It's designed for building interactive dashboards with ease.
   - **Use Cases:** Interactive data visualization, creating web applications.
8. **Dask:**
   - **Key Features:** Dask is a library for parallel and distributed computing in Python. It allows you to work with larger-than-memory datasets and perform parallel operations, making it

suitable for big data manipulation.
- **Use Cases:** Scalable data processing, parallel computing, handling large datasets.

9. **polars:**
   - **Key Features:** polars is a DataFrame library designed for high-performance data manipulation. It offers similar functionality to pandas but with a focus on speed and scalability.
   - **Use Cases:** Fast data manipulation, large-scale data analysis.

10. **Vaex:**
    - **Key Features:** Vaex is a library for lazy, out-of-core DataFrames. It's designed to handle extremely large datasets efficiently by only loading the data into memory when needed.
    - **Use Cases:** Handling massive datasets, out-of-core data processing.

These libraries are commonly used in various data-related tasks, from data cleaning and preprocessing to visualization and analysis. Depending on your specific data manipulation needs and preferences, you can choose the library that best suits your project and workflow.

Describe the significance of NumPy and how to use it.

NumPy (Numerical Python) is a fundamental library in the Python ecosystem for numerical and scientific computing. It provides essential tools and data structures for working with arrays and matrices, making it a cornerstone for tasks involving numerical operations, data manipulation, and scientific computing. Here's a breakdown of the significance of NumPy and how to use it:

Significance of NumPy:

1. **Efficient Data Storage:** NumPy introduces the **ndarray** (n-dimensional array) data structure, which is highly efficient for storing and manipulating large datasets. It stores homogeneous data types, allowing for memory-efficient storage and fast data access.

2. **Vectorized Operations:** NumPy allows you to perform element-wise operations on entire arrays, eliminating the need for explicit loops in your code. This vectorization significantly improves

performance and code readability.

3. **Broad Numeric Support:** NumPy provides support for a wide range of numeric data types, including integers, floats, complex numbers, and more. This versatility is essential for scientific computing and data analysis.

4. **Mathematical Functions:** NumPy includes a comprehensive library of mathematical functions for common operations like addition, subtraction, multiplication, and advanced functions such as trigonometric, exponential, and logarithmic functions.

5. **Broadcasting:** NumPy's broadcasting feature enables you to work with arrays of different shapes in a natural and efficient way. It automatically aligns and extends smaller arrays to match the shape of larger arrays for element-wise operations.

6. **Interoperability:** NumPy seamlessly integrates with other scientific libraries and tools, such as SciPy (for scientific computing), Matplotlib (for data visualization), and pandas (for data manipulation).

How to Use NumPy:

To start using NumPy, you typically follow these steps:

1. **Installation:** NumPy is not included in the Python standard library, so you need to install it separately. You can use a package manager like **pip** or **conda** to install NumPy:

```
pip install numpy
```

2. **Import NumPy:** In your Python script or notebook, import the NumPy library using the **import** statement:

```
import numpy as np
```

It's a common convention to alias NumPy as **np** for brevity.

3. **Creating Arrays:** You can create NumPy arrays in various ways:
   - From Python lists or tuples:

```
my_array = np.array([1, 2, 3, 4, 5])
```

   - Using NumPy functions like **np.zeros()**, **np.ones()**, **np.arange()**, and **np.linspace()**.
   - Reading data from external sources like CSV files using

np.genfromtxt() or **np.loadtxt()**.

4. **Array Operations:** NumPy arrays support a wide range of operations:
   - Element-wise arithmetic operations:

result = array1 + array2

   - Mathematical functions:

result = np.sin(array)

   - Slicing and indexing:

subset = array[1:4]

   - Aggregation and reduction:

mean = np.mean(array)

5. **Broadcasting:** Take advantage of NumPy's broadcasting to perform operations on arrays with different shapes while maintaining code simplicity.
6. **Advanced Features:** Explore NumPy's advanced features, including random number generation (**np.random**), linear algebra operations (**np.linalg**), and more specialized functions for your specific needs.
7. **Visualization:** You can visualize data in NumPy arrays using libraries like Matplotlib or Seaborn. These libraries work seamlessly with NumPy to create insightful visualizations.

Here's a simple example of creating NumPy arrays and performing basic operations:

```
import numpy as np

# Create NumPy arrays
array1 = np.array([1, 2, 3, 4, 5])
array2 = np.array([5, 4, 3, 2, 1])

# Perform element-wise operations
```

```
sum_result = array1 + array2
product_result = array1 * array2

# Calculate the mean
mean = np.mean(array1)

print("Sum Result:", sum_result)
print("Product Result:", product_result)
print("Mean:", mean)
```

In this example, NumPy simplifies array creation and enables efficient element-wise operations and aggregation, making it a powerful tool for numerical computing and scientific tasks. Its versatility and performance make it a cornerstone of the Python data science ecosystem.

Explain the role of pandas in data analysis.

pandas is a powerful and widely used Python library for data analysis and manipulation. It plays a central role in the data science and data analysis workflows. Here's an explanation of the role of pandas in data analysis:

1. **Data Structure:** At the core of pandas is the DataFrame data structure. A DataFrame is a two-dimensional, table-like data structure that allows you to store and manipulate structured data efficiently. It is similar to a spreadsheet or SQL table.

2. **Data Cleaning and Preprocessing:** pandas provides a wide range of functions and methods for cleaning and preprocessing data. These include functions for handling missing data, removing duplicates, and transforming data types.

3. **Data Exploration:** Data scientists and analysts often start their analysis by exploring the dataset. pandas simplifies this process with functions for basic statistics (**describe()**), summarization, and visualization (integration with Matplotlib and Seaborn). You can quickly get insights into the data's distribution, central tendencies, and variability.

4. **Data Filtering and Selection:** pandas allows you to filter and select data based on various conditions and criteria. You can perform operations like selecting rows and columns by label or position, filtering based on conditions, and chaining operations to

refine the selection.

5. **Data Aggregation and Grouping:** pandas makes it easy to perform aggregation operations on data. You can group data by one or more columns and then apply aggregation functions like sum, mean, median, or custom functions to obtain summarized information.

6. **Data Transformation:** Data often requires transformation before analysis or modeling. pandas provides powerful tools for reshaping data, such as pivoting, melting, and stacking/unstacking. You can also merge and concatenate DataFrames.

7. **Time Series Analysis:** pandas excels in time series analysis with specialized data structures like the **DateTimeIndex**. It includes functions for resampling, rolling calculations, and handling time-based data efficiently.

8. **Integration with Data Sources:** pandas can read data from various sources, including CSV, Excel, SQL databases, and web APIs. It simplifies data ingestion and allows you to work with data from diverse sources seamlessly.

9. **Handling Categorical Data:** Categorical data can be challenging to work with, but pandas provides tools for encoding and handling categorical variables, making them suitable for machine learning and analysis.

10. **Data Visualization:** While pandas itself is not a visualization library, it integrates seamlessly with data visualization libraries like Matplotlib and Seaborn. You can create insightful charts and plots directly from pandas DataFrames.

11. **Exporting Data:** After data analysis and manipulation, you can easily export the processed data to various formats, such as CSV, Excel, or SQL databases, using pandas functions.

12. **Data Analysis Workflows:** pandas is an integral part of data analysis workflows. It is often used in conjunction with other libraries like NumPy, scikit-learn (for machine learning), Matplotlib, and Jupyter notebooks to create end-to-end data analysis pipelines.

13. **Interactive Data Exploration:** pandas can be used interactively in Jupyter notebooks, enabling users to explore data step by step and share insights through interactive reports.

14. **Data Cleaning and Transformation Automation:** pandas

allows you to automate repetitive data cleaning and transformation tasks, reducing the need for manual intervention and improving data consistency.

What is Django, and how is it used for web development?

Django is a high-level, open-source Python web framework that simplifies and accelerates the development of web applications. It follows the "batteries-included" philosophy, providing a comprehensive set of tools and features for building robust and scalable web applications. Here's an overview of what Django is and how it is used for web development:

Key Features of Django:

1. **Model-View-Controller (MVC) Architecture:** Django follows the Model-View-Controller architectural pattern, but in Django, it's often referred to as the Model-View-Template (MVT) pattern. This separation of concerns promotes clean code and maintainability.

2. **Database Abstraction:** Django includes its Object-Relational Mapping (ORM) system, allowing developers to define data models using Python classes. This abstraction simplifies database operations and supports multiple database backends.

3. **Admin Interface:** Django provides an automatically generated admin interface. This admin panel allows you to manage data, users, and content without building a custom administrative system.

4. **URL Routing:** Django's URL routing system allows you to map URLs to specific views and functions. This makes it easy to define the structure of your web application.

5. **Template Engine:** Django includes a template system that separates HTML code from Python logic. It enables the creation of dynamic and reusable templates for rendering web pages.

6. **Form Handling:** Django simplifies form handling, validation, and rendering. It includes tools for building forms and processing form submissions securely.

7. **Authentication and Authorization:** Django offers robust authentication and authorization mechanisms, including user management, permissions, and security features like protection

against common web vulnerabilities.

8. **Security Features:** Django is designed with security in mind. It provides built-in protection against common web vulnerabilities, such as Cross-Site Scripting (XSS) and Cross-Site Request Forgery (CSRF).

9. **Session Management:** Django handles user sessions and cookies out of the box, making it straightforward to manage user state.

10. **Internationalization and Localization:** Django supports internationalization (i18n) and localization (l10n), making it possible to create applications that cater to a global audience.

11. **Middleware:** Middleware components can be added to Django to perform various tasks, such as authentication, logging, and request/response processing.

12. **Reusable Apps:** Django encourages the creation of reusable applications that can be easily integrated into different projects. The Django community offers a vast ecosystem of third-party apps.

How Django Is Used for Web Development:

1. **Project Setup:** To start a Django project, you use the Django command-line tools to create a project structure. This structure includes settings, URLs, and application management.

2. **Defining Models:** In Django, you define your data models using Python classes. These models represent database tables and can include relationships between tables.

3. **Creating Views:** Django views are Python functions or classes that handle HTTP requests. They process data, interact with the database, and return responses.

4. **Defining URLs:** URL routing maps URLs to views. In the project's URL configuration, you specify which view should handle each URL pattern.

5. **Creating Templates:** Django templates are used to render HTML dynamically. You define templates that can include placeholders for dynamic content.

6. **Form Handling:** Django simplifies form handling by providing form classes and validation mechanisms. Forms can be used to receive and process user input.

7. **Admin Panel:** The admin interface is automatically generated based on your data models. It allows administrators to manage

application data without writing custom admin code.

8. **Authentication and Authorization:** Django provides built-in authentication and authorization features. You can control user access to various parts of your application.

9. **Testing:** Django includes a testing framework for writing and running unit tests, making it easier to ensure the correctness of your code.

10. **Deployment:** Django applications can be deployed to various hosting platforms, including cloud services and traditional web servers. Popular deployment options include using WSGI servers like Gunicorn and web servers like Apache or Nginx.

11. **Scaling:** Django applications can be scaled horizontally and vertically to handle increased traffic and demand. Options for scaling include load balancing, database replication, and caching.

Discuss the importance of Flask in web application development.

Flask is a lightweight and flexible micro web framework for Python, and it plays a significant role in web application development. While not as feature-rich as some larger web frameworks like Django, Flask offers simplicity, versatility, and a minimalistic approach that makes it invaluable for various web development scenarios. Here's a discussion of the importance of Flask in web application development:

1. **Simplicity and Minimalism:** Flask is designed with simplicity in mind. Its core is minimal, providing only essential components for building web applications. This minimalistic approach allows developers to have more control over their code, making it easier to understand and maintain.

2. **Flexibility:** Flask doesn't impose rigid structures or conventions on developers. This flexibility means you can choose the libraries and tools you want to use, allowing for a custom stack that fits your project's specific needs.

3. **Easy to Learn:** Flask's minimalistic design makes it one of the easiest web frameworks to learn, especially for developers who are new to web development. Its small codebase and straightforward documentation enable quick onboarding.

4. **Rapid Prototyping:** Flask is ideal for rapid prototyping and

building small to medium-sized web applications quickly. Its simplicity and minimal setup overhead allow developers to focus on functionality and features.

5. **RESTful APIs:** Flask is a popular choice for building RESTful APIs. Its lightweight nature and support for HTTP methods make it well-suited for creating backend APIs that serve data to front-end applications.

6. **Extensions and Libraries:** Flask has a rich ecosystem of extensions and libraries, known as Flask extensions, that can be easily integrated to add functionality. These extensions cover areas like authentication, database integration, form handling, and more.

7. **Testing and Debugging:** Flask provides robust support for unit testing and debugging. The built-in development server has debugging features, and testing Flask applications is straightforward, facilitating test-driven development (TDD).

8. **Scalability:** While Flask is often used for small to medium-sized projects, it can be scaled for larger applications by adding extensions and structuring the code appropriately. Flask's simplicity allows for a gradual transition as projects grow.

9. **Community and Documentation:** Flask has an active and supportive community. The official documentation is well-maintained and comprehensive, making it easy to find answers to questions and troubleshoot issues.

10. **Microservices:** Flask's lightweight nature and ease of creating RESTful APIs make it a popular choice for building microservices within a larger architecture. It can seamlessly integrate with other services and technologies.

11. **Deployment:** Deploying Flask applications is straightforward. Flask can be hosted on various platforms, including traditional web servers, cloud platforms, and containerized environments.

12. **Educational Value:** Flask is often used in educational settings and tutorials due to its simplicity and transparency. It's an excellent choice for teaching web development concepts to beginners.

13. **Prototyping for Larger Projects:** Developers often use Flask to prototype ideas before committing to a larger framework like Django or a full-stack JavaScript framework. Flask allows you to validate concepts quickly.

ADVANCED TOPICS

What are decorators, and how do you use them in Python?

Decorators are a powerful and flexible feature in Python that allow you to modify or enhance the behavior of functions or methods without changing their core code. Decorators are commonly used for tasks such as logging, authentication, measuring execution time, and more. They provide a way to wrap or "decorate" functions with additional functionality. Decorators are defined using the **@** symbol followed by the decorator function name, placed above the function definition.

Here's a basic explanation of decorators and how to use them in Python:

Defining a Decorator Function:

To create a decorator, you define a regular Python function that takes another function as its argument. This decorator function can perform actions before and after calling the original function it decorates. Here's a simple example of a decorator function:

```
def my_decorator(func):
    def wrapper():
        print("Something is happening before the function is called.")
        func()
```

```
    print("Something is happening after the function is called.")
    return wrapper
```

In this example, **my_decorator** is a decorator function that takes **func** as its argument. Inside **my_decorator**, there's an inner function called **wrapper**, which calls **func** and adds custom behavior before and after the function call.

Applying a Decorator:

To apply a decorator to a function, you use the **@** symbol followed by the decorator function name, placed above the function definition. Here's an example of applying the **my_decorator** to a simple function:

```
@my_decorator
def say_hello():
    print("Hello!")

# Calling the decorated function
say_hello()
```

When you call **say_hello()**, the decorator **my_decorator** modifies the behavior of the **say_hello** function. It adds the custom messages before and after the function's execution.

Output:

```
Something is happening before the function is called.
Hello!
Something is happening after the function is called.
```

Common Use Cases for Decorators:
1. **Logging:** You can create decorators to log function calls and their arguments, making it easier to debug and monitor your code.
2. **Authentication:** Decorators can check user authentication or permissions before allowing access to certain routes or functions in a web application.
3. **Caching:** Decorators can be used to cache the results of expensive function calls, improving performance.
4. **Timing:** You can measure the execution time of functions

using decorators for profiling and optimization.

5. **Validation:** Decorators can validate input arguments before executing a function.
6. **Authorization:** Decorators can ensure that a user has the necessary privileges to perform a specific action.
7. **Route Handling (Web Frameworks):** In web frameworks like Flask or Django, decorators are used to define routes and specify additional functionality for view functions.
8. **Method Wrapping:** Decorators can modify the behavior of methods in classes, allowing you to implement features like memoization or data validation for object methods.

Decorators are a powerful tool in Python that promote code reusability, modularity, and maintainability. They are commonly used in web frameworks, testing frameworks, and various other Python libraries to extend and customize functionality. Understanding decorators is essential for becoming proficient in Python programming.

Explain the concept of generators and iterators.

Generators and **iterators** are related concepts in Python that deal with the iteration over sequences of data. They allow you to work with large datasets or infinite sequences of data efficiently, without loading everything into memory at once. However, they serve slightly different purposes.

Iterators:

An **iterator** is an object that implements two methods: **__iter__()** and **__next__()**. These methods are used to iterate over a sequence of items one at a time. Here's how they work:

- **__iter__()**: This method returns the iterator object itself. It is called when you initiate an iteration.
- **__next__()**: This method retrieves the next item from the iterator. If there are no more items, it raises the **StopIteration** exception to signal the end of the iteration.

Here's a simple example of an iterator:

```
class MyIterator:
    def __init__(self, data):
        self.data = data
        self.index = 0
```

```
def __iter__(self):
    return self

def __next__(self):
    if self.index >= len(self.data):
        raise StopIteration
    item = self.data[self.index]
    self.index += 1
    return item

# Usage:
my_list = [1, 2, 3, 4, 5]
my_iterator = MyIterator(my_list)

for item in my_iterator:
    print(item)
```

Generators:

A **generator** is a special type of iterator created using a function rather than a class. It uses the **yield** keyword to produce values one at a time. When a function contains a **yield** statement, it becomes a generator function, and calling it doesn't execute the function; instead, it returns a generator object.

Here's an example of a generator function:

```
def my_generator(data):
    for item in data:
        yield item

# Usage:
my_list = [1, 2, 3, 4, 5]
gen = my_generator(my_list)

for item in gen:
    print(item)
```

The key difference between iterators and generators is that generators are more memory-efficient because they produce values on-the-fly and don't store the entire sequence in memory. They are particularly useful for large datasets or infinite sequences.

Use Cases:

- **Iterators:** You might implement an iterator when you have a specific use case that requires custom logic for iterating over data. This could be for iterating over files, databases, or other non-standard data sources.

- **Generators:** Generators are typically preferred when you want to create an iterable sequence without loading all the data into memory. This is common when processing large datasets, reading data from external sources, or working with infinite sequences (e.g., streaming data).

In practice, Python provides built-in functions like **range()**, **map()**, and **filter()** that return iterators, and list comprehensions that implicitly use iterators. Additionally, many Python libraries and functions return or accept iterators and generators, making them an integral part of Python's iterative programming paradigm.

How does multithreading work in Python?

Multithreading in Python allows you to create and manage multiple threads within a single process. Threads are lightweight, independently executing units of a program that can run concurrently. Multithreading is beneficial for tasks that can be parallelized, such as I/O-bound operations or tasks that require periodic execution in the background.

Python provides a built-in module called **threading** for working with threads. Here's an overview of how multithreading works in Python:

1. **Importing the threading Module:**

To use multithreading in Python, you need to import the **threading** module.

```
import threading
```

2. **Creating Threads:**

You can create threads by defining a function and then creating thread objects that execute that function. Here's an example:

```
import threading
```

```
def my_function():
    print("This is a thread.")

# Create two threads
thread1 = threading.Thread(target=my_function)
thread2 = threading.Thread(target=my_function)
```

3. **Starting Threads:**
To start a thread, you call the **start()** method on the thread object:

```
thread1.start()
thread2.start()
```

This initiates the execution of the **my_function()** in each thread concurrently.

4. **Joining Threads:**
You can use the **join()** method to wait for a thread to complete its execution before continuing with the main thread. This is useful when you want to ensure that all threads have finished before proceeding.

```
thread1.join()
thread2.join()
```

5. **Thread Safety:**
When working with multithreaded applications, you should be aware of thread safety. This means ensuring that shared resources (like variables or data structures) are accessed and modified in a thread-safe manner to avoid data corruption or unexpected behavior. You can use locks (**threading.Lock**) or other synchronization mechanisms to protect critical sections of your code.

Here's a complete example demonstrating the basic usage of multithreading in Python:

```
import threading

def print_numbers():
    for i in range(1, 6):
```

```python
    print(f"Number: {i}")

def print_letters():
    for letter in "abcde":
        print(f"Letter: {letter}")

# Create two threads
thread1 = threading.Thread(target=print_numbers)
thread2 = threading.Thread(target=print_letters)

# Start the threads
thread1.start()
thread2.start()

# Wait for both threads to finish
thread1.join()
thread2.join()

print("Both threads have finished.")
```

In this example, **print_numbers** and **print_letters** are two functions running in separate threads concurrently.

It's important to note that Python's Global Interpreter Lock (GIL) can limit the true parallel execution of threads in CPython, the default Python interpreter. GIL ensures that only one thread executes Python bytecode at a time. While multithreading can still be useful in Python for I/O-bound tasks and managing concurrent tasks, it may not provide the same level of performance improvement as it would in languages without a GIL. For CPU-bound tasks that require true parallelism, consider using multiprocessing or other parallel processing techniques.

Describe the use of virtual environments.

Virtual environments are isolated environments that allow you to manage Python packages and dependencies for different projects separately. They are essential tools in Python development to avoid conflicts between packages, versions, and dependencies when working on multiple projects. Here's a detailed description of the use of virtual environments:

Why Use Virtual Environments?
1. **Isolation:** Virtual environments provide isolation between different Python projects. Each environment has its own isolated set of Python packages and dependencies, ensuring that changes in one project don't affect others.
2. **Version Control:** Virtual environments enable you to control the version of Python used for a project. You can create environments for different Python versions, ensuring compatibility with your code.
3. **Dependency Management:** When working on projects with different requirements, you can define and manage project-specific dependencies easily. This avoids conflicts and keeps dependencies organized.
4. **Cleaner Development:** Virtual environments keep your global Python installation clean. You can install packages in project-specific environments without cluttering your system-wide Python installation.

Using Virtual Environments:
1. **Create a Virtual Environment:**
To create a virtual environment, you use Python's built-in module called **venv** (or **virtualenv** if you prefer a third-party package). Navigate to your project directory and run:

```
python -m venv myenv
```

Replace **myenv** with your preferred environment name.
2. **Activate the Virtual Environment:**
After creating a virtual environment, you need to activate it. On Windows, you can use:

```
myenv\Scripts\activate
```

On macOS and Linux, use:
bashCopy code
source myenv/bin/activate
When the environment is activated, your shell prompt will change to indicate the active environment.
3. **Install Packages:**
With the virtual environment activated, you can install packages

using **pip**. For example:

pip install package_name

This installs packages within the active environment.

4. **Deactivate the Environment:**

When you're done working on your project, you can deactivate the virtual environment:

deactivate

This returns you to the global Python environment.

5. **Requirements File:**

It's a good practice to create a **requirements.txt** file in your project directory listing all the dependencies and their versions. You can generate this file using:

pip freeze > requirements.txt

Then, to recreate the environment with the same dependencies, you can use:

pip install -r requirements.txt

6. **Removing a Virtual Environment:**

If you no longer need a virtual environment, you can simply delete its directory. Be cautious when doing this to avoid accidental data loss.

Use Cases for Virtual Environments:

- **Web Development:** Virtual environments are commonly used for web development projects, where each web application or website is developed in a separate environment.
- **Data Science:** Data scientists use virtual environments to manage dependencies for different data analysis projects.
- **Testing:** Creating isolated environments for testing ensures that test cases don't interfere with each other and produce consistent results.
- **Python Package Development:** When developing Python packages, it's essential to test them in clean, isolated

environments to ensure they work correctly with different dependencies.

What are some best practices for writing efficient Python code?

Writing efficient Python code is crucial for ensuring that your programs run smoothly, consume fewer resources, and perform well. Here are some best practices for writing efficient Python code:

1. **Use Built-In Functions and Libraries:**
   - Python's standard library includes many built-in functions and modules optimized for efficiency. Utilize them whenever possible, as they are typically faster than implementing custom solutions.
   - Examples include **len()**, **range()**, **map()**, **filter()**, and **collections** modules (e.g., **collections.Counter** for counting elements).

2. **Avoid Using Global Variables:**
   - Minimize the use of global variables. Accessing global variables is slower than accessing local ones, as Python has to search through multiple scopes.
   - If you need shared data, consider using function arguments or returning values instead.

3. **Use List Comprehensions:**
   - List comprehensions are more efficient and concise than traditional **for** loops for creating lists. They also offer better performance due to their optimized implementation.

4. **Generator Expressions:**
   - When dealing with large datasets, prefer generator expressions over lists. They generate values on-the-fly, saving memory and improving performance.
   - Use parentheses instead of brackets to create generator expressions.

5. **Avoid Unnecessary Loops:**
   - Reduce the number of loops whenever possible. Nested loops, in particular, can lead to poor performance.
   - Consider using vectorized operations with libraries like NumPy for array operations.

6. **Optimize String Concatenation:**
    - String concatenation can be slow, especially inside loops. Instead of repeatedly concatenating strings, use **str.join()** to concatenate a list of strings.
    - For frequent string modifications, consider using the **str.join()** approach along with the **str.split()** and **str.replace()** methods.
7. **Choose the Right Data Structures:**
    - Select the appropriate data structure for your specific use case. For example, use sets for membership tests, dictionaries for fast lookups, and lists for ordered collections.
    - Research and understand the time complexity of operations on different data structures.
8. **Profile and Optimize:**
    - Use profiling tools like **cProfile** or **line_profiler** to identify bottlenecks in your code.
    - Optimize the most time-consuming parts of your code, but avoid premature optimization. Focus on areas that truly impact performance.
9. **Cache Results:**
    - If a function produces the same output for the same input multiple times, consider caching the results to avoid redundant computations. Python provides tools like **functools.lru_cache** for this purpose.
10. **Avoid Using global Keyword:**
    - Minimize the use of the **global** keyword, as it can lead to performance issues and make code harder to maintain. Instead, pass variables as arguments or return values from functions.
11. **Use if __name__ == "__main__": for Script Execution:**
    - When writing scripts, use the **if __name__ == "__main__":** construct to ensure that code in the script is executed only when the script is run as the main program. This prevents executing unnecessary code when the script is imported as a module.
12. **Document Your Code:**
    - Well-documented code is easier to understand and maintain. Use docstrings and comments to explain the

purpose of functions, classes, and complex algorithms.

13. **Profile Memory Usage:**
    - Besides profiling CPU usage, consider profiling memory usage using tools like **memory_profiler** to identify and optimize memory-intensive parts of your code.

14. **Use Efficient Algorithms:**
    - Choose efficient algorithms and data structures for specific tasks. Understanding algorithmic complexity (Big O notation) helps in selecting the right approach.

15. **Keep an Eye on I/O Operations:**
    - I/O operations (e.g., reading/writing files, network requests) are often the bottleneck in a program. Optimize I/O-bound operations by using buffering and asynchronous techniques.

16. **Stay Informed:**
    - Keep up-to-date with Python releases and best practices. Python evolves, and newer versions may offer performance improvements and optimizations.

CONCLUSION

Preparing for Your Python Interview

Preparing for a Python interview requires a combination of understanding the language fundamentals, practicing coding exercises, and being prepared to answer technical questions. Here's a step-by-step guide to help you prepare effectively:

1. **Review Python Fundamentals:**

   - Ensure you have a strong grasp of Python's fundamental concepts, including data types, variables, operators, and control flow structures (if statements, loops, etc.).

2. **Data Structures and Algorithms:**

   - Study common data structures (lists, dictionaries, sets, etc.) and algorithms (sorting, searching, etc.) and understand their time and space complexities.

3. **Object-Oriented Programming (OOP):**

   - Familiarize yourself with OOP principles, including classes, objects, inheritance, polymorphism, and encapsulation.

4. **Exception Handling:**

   - Understand how to handle exceptions using **try, except, finally,** and **raise.** Be prepared to explain error-handling strategies.

5. **File Handling:**

   - Learn how to open, read, and write files in Python.

Understand different file modes and how to work with file paths.

6. **Modules and Libraries:**

   - Explore commonly used Python libraries and modules, such as **os**, **sys**, **math**, and third-party libraries like NumPy, pandas, Flask, and Django.

7. **Decorators and Generators:**

   - Understand the concepts of decorators and generators and how to use them in Python.

8. **Basic SQL (for Data Science roles):**

   - If you're interviewing for data science roles, review basic SQL queries for data manipulation.

9. **Practice Coding:**

   - Solve coding challenges on platforms like LeetCode, HackerRank, and CodeSignal. Focus on a variety of topics, including data structures, algorithms, and problem-solving.

10. **Review Projects:**

    - If you have personal or open-source Python projects, be prepared to discuss them. Explain the problem you solved, your approach, and any challenges you faced.

11. **Practice Whiteboard Coding (if applicable):**

    - If your interview includes whiteboard coding, practice solving problems on a whiteboard or paper to simulate the interview environment.

12. Behavioral Questions:

- Prepare for behavioral questions that assess your soft skills, teamwork, communication, and problem-solving abilities. Use the STAR (Situation, Task, Action, Result) method to structure your answers.

13. Ask Questions:

- Prepare thoughtful questions to ask the interviewer. Questions about the company, team, and the role demonstrate your interest and engagement.

14. Mock Interviews:

- Conduct mock interviews with peers or mentors to simulate the interview experience. Request feedback on your coding and communication skills.

15. Stay Updated:

- Stay up-to-date with Python updates and best practices. Python evolves, and interviewers may ask about the latest features or improvements.

16. Review the Job Description:

- Analyze the job description to understand the specific skills and qualifications the company is looking for. Tailor your preparation accordingly.

17. Relax and Stay Calm:

- On the interview day, remain calm and confident. Remember that interviews are not only about the right answers but also about problem-solving skills, communication, and your ability to learn and adapt.

18. Follow-Up:

- After the interview, send a thank-you email to express your gratitude for the opportunity and reiterate your interest in the position.

By following these steps and dedicating time to study and practice, you can approach your Python interview with confidence and increase your chances of success. Remember that interview performance is a combination of technical knowledge, problem-solving skills, and effective communication. Good luck!

www.ingramcontent.com/pod-product-compliance
Lightning Source LLC
Chambersburg PA
CBHW050735260726

48661CB00001B/245